Caronia passing the Statue of Liberty, New York.

Right: Cunard advertisement, 1948.

led by the

Cunard White Star sailings are fast resuming pre-war frequency.

The *Queen Elizabeth* and *Queen Mary*, supported by the *Mauretania*, provide superlative travel comfort on the express service — Southampton, Cherbourg and New York.

On the Liverpool-New York run, the newly-reconditioned *Britannic*, calling regularly at Cobh, operates with two of the new Atlantic liners, *Media* and *Parthia*.

Atlantic

Canada is served by the *Aquitania* from Southampton and the *Ascania* from Liverpool, providing especially for emigrants.

And now the *Caronia* — Britain's new wonder ship, makes her maiden voyage from Southampton, via Cherbourg, to New York on 4th Jan., 1949.

Queens

For full information apply Liverpool 3: Pier Head (Central 9201). London S.W.1.: 15 Lower Regent St. (Whitehall 7890). London E.C.3.: 88 Leadenhall St. (Avenue 3010), or principal travel agencies.

Cunard White Star

Her Royal Highness Princess Elizabeth launched the Cunard liner *Caronia* on 30 October 1947, at the yard of John Brown & Co. on the River Clyde. *Caronia* was designed as a dual-purpose vessel to operate on transatlantic crossings and cruising duties. It was originally envisaged that she would be a sister to *Mauretania*, which had been completed by Cammell Laird at Birkenhead in 1939. They were described as 'intermediate' vessels that would substitute for the two Queens when required, and be able to maintain the transatlantic schedules. *Mauretania* was only able to complete two transatlantic crossings before she was requisitioned for service in the Second World War as a troop carrier.

At the end of the war, *Mauretania* was returned to service and the Cunard Board decided that *Caronia* would be built and employed in the cruise market, but able to provide transatlantic crossings. Consequently, she was built with a swimming pool, and provided bathroom/shower facilities in each cabin; she was designed as a two-class liner, first and cabin for the transatlantic service. While on cruising duties she operated as a one-class vessel.

She was described as 'a distinguished example of naval architecture that reaches a combination of technical and artistic achievement unsurpassed in British shipbuilding'. Her public rooms embraced a verandah café, observation lounge, cocktail bar, lounge, writing room, smoking room, library, theatre, gymnasium, two garden lounges, and an aft cocktail bar and smoking room. Nearly all bedrooms were outside, with portholes or windows, and the ship was served by over 570 clocks. She was fitted with six diesel-engine covered passenger launches on the boat deck, which were rated as lifeboats and used to transport passengers between ship and shore.

Caronia sailed on her maiden voyage on 4 January 1949 from Southampton to New York with her hull painted in various shades of green, and was soon referred to as the 'Green Goddess', a name she retained during her career with the Cunard Line. The following month she embarked on her first cruise season, sailing from New York to the Caribbean, and returned to the North Atlantic service in April that year for the summer.

Her first major cruise was 'The Great African Cruise', which took her from New York on 12 January 1950 to Trinidad, Bahia, Rio de Janeiro, Tristan da Cunha, Cape Town, Durban, Mombasa, Suez Canal, Israel, Greece, Algiers, Gibraltar, Portugal, Cherbourg and Southampton. Passengers then returned to New York on one of the Queen liners. *Caronia* made her first World Cruise the following year, sailing via the Panama Canal to Acapulco, Los Angeles, New Zealand, Australia, Singapore, Colombo, Bombay, Aden, Suez Canal, Israel, Greece, Italy, Gibraltar, Lisbon, Cherbourg and Southampton. Although the cruise was not fully booked, she proved herself as a popular, modern and successful luxury cruise liner, and a true pioneer of sea travel for the future.

Caronia was conceived and built at a time when British shipping lines provided a network of scheduled liner services around the globe, and were also seeing the advantages of providing employment for their passenger ships during the winter months. Cruising, especially from American ports, had been a dollar earner for many of the British companies in the 1920s and 1930s, as the Cunard Line, Canadian Pacific and several other British lines found when they sent their vessels to offer cruises from the United States.

However, at the time of *Caronia*'s maiden voyage, the British shipping lines were engaged in rebuilding their fleets, which had been decimated during the hostilities of the Second World War. Cunard Line had lost *Andania*, *Bosnia*, *Carinthia*, *Laconia*, *Lancastria* and *Laurentic*. *Antonia* had become HMS *Wayland*, *Aurania* was converted to HMS *Artifax*, and *Alaunia* and *Ausonia* were renamed HMS *Alaunia* and HMS *Ausonia*. Canadian Pacific Steamships lost *Empress of Britain* in 1940, *Empress of Asia* was sunk at Singapore in 1942 and *Duchess of Athol* was torpedoed west of Ascension Island by the German submarine U-178. *Duchess of York* was lost in 1943 after being bombed by German aircraft. Blue Star Line's

Almeda Star was sunk by a torpedo in 1941, west of the Outer Hebrides. *Andalucia Star* was torpedoed and sunk on 7 October 1942, *Arandora Star* was torpedoed and sank in just over an hour on 3 June 1940, *Avelona Star* was lost off Cape Finisterre in 1940, and *Avila Star* was torpedoed and sank west of the Azores on 6 July 1942.

The experience of shipping lines using their vessels for cruising prior to the Second World War was clearly an advantage in designing replacement ships for those lost between 1939 and 1945. Although built in 1939, *Queen Elizabeth* was converted back from her wartime role as a troop carrier, and sailed on her first commercial voyage for the Cunard Line on 16 October 1946. She was joined by *Queen Mary* on the Southampton–New York service, and *Mauretania* resumed the Liverpool–New York service on 26 April 1947, before she was later based at Southampton. *Mauretania* operated cruises out of New York between January and March the following year.

Cunard's replacement plans lasted for twelve years and included the building of the cargo/passenger liners *Media* and *Parthia* and replacing *Ascania*, *Franconia*, *Samaria* and *Scythia*. The new vessels for the Canadian service were *Saxonia*, *Ivernia*, *Carinthia* and later *Sylvania*. By 1960 the Cunard Line operated ten passenger ships. Canadian Pacific acquired the *De Grasse* in 1953 to replace the fire-damaged *Empress of Canada*, and renamed her *Empress of Australia*. They introduced the new *Empress of Britain* in 1956, *Empress of England* the following year and *Empress of Canada* in 1961.

The other main shipping companies were also replacing older tonnage that had survived wartime service to the country. P&O's *Himalaya* was delivered in 1949, *Chusan* in 1950, *Arcadia* and *Iberia* in 1954 and *Canberra* in 1961. Orient Lines' *Orcades* was built in 1948, *Oronsay* in 1951, *Orsova* in 1954, with their replacement programme culminating in the maiden voyage to Australia, New Zealand, Vancouver and San Francisco of *Oriana* on 3 December 1960, which followed a short cruise to Lisbon with the Association of British Travel Agents.

Lamport & Holt decided not to replace their cruise ships *Vandyck* and *Voltaire*, which had been lost in 1940 and 1941 respectively. The Blue Star Line ordered *Argentina Star*, *Brazil Star*, *Uruguay Star* and *Paraguay Star*, which were able to carry sixty first-class passengers in single and double cabins on their service from London to Lisbon, Tenerife, Rio de Janeiro, Santos, Montevideo and Buenos Aires.

Furness Withy's *Queen of Bermuda* was fitted with air conditioning during her major overhaul in 1947, and returned to the New York–Bermuda sailings on 12 February 1949, with accommodation for 682 first- and 49 second-class passengers. Her sister, *Monarch of Bermuda*, had been almost destroyed by fire during her overhaul in 1947, and was acquired by the Ministry of Transport and rebuilt as an emigrant carrier for the United Kingdom–Australia route. The company decided to replace her, and *Ocean Monarch* was ordered from Vickers Armstrong Limited at Newcastle, taking her first sailing from New York on 3 May 1951, with 414 first-class passengers on board. She had been designed as a smaller vessel than the *Monarch of Bermuda* as it was realised as early as that time that the route was beginning to feel the competition from the airlines.

Britannic, which was built in 1930, was the last surviving member of the White Star Line, and had spent the war years operating as a troopship. At the end of hostilities she had carried 180,000 troops and steamed 376,000 miles, and was finally returned to the Cunard-White Star Line in 1947. She resumed commercial service on the Liverpool–New York run the following year and was also employed in cruising duties from the United States. Her sister *Georgic* was less fortunate, as she had been seriously damaged in 1941 by German aircraft when she was at anchor at Port Tewfik in the Gulf of Suez. She was eventually brought home to Belfast where she was repaired and continued trooping duties until the end of the war. She continued in service on the Australia and New Zealand emigrant trade, and was briefly chartered back to the Cunard Line in the early 1950s for the Liverpool–

New York and Southampton–New York services. Following the completion of these charters she was offered for sale, and following a charter to the Australian government she was sold and broken up in 1956.

In the early 1960s, prior to the maiden voyage of *Northern Star*, Lord Sanderson, Chairman of the Shaw Savill Line, recognised the problem of the cargo and passenger mix in the design of new vessels. He said,

> In the years since 1945 it has become evident that it is often unsatisfactory to carry large cargoes and a given number of passengers in the same vessel. Changing conditions in the loading and discharge of cargo have led to longer periods in ports abroad with crews on articles, most of whom are engaged to attend to the needs of passengers, while it is invariably the cargo which is responsible for the delays and longer voyage.

He said that those factors influenced the Shaw Savill Line in their decision to build a purely passenger ship carrying no cargo whatsoever, which could make four round voyages a year to New Zealand, Australia and South Africa, instead of fewer than three voyages possible in the same time in a passenger/cargo vessel.

He explained that the decision made it possible for them to depart from the conventional in the internal design of the ship. The absence of cargo hatches in the passenger decks facilitated the layout of both public rooms and cabins, but there still remained the obstructions of engine room casings and the funnel uptakes, which normally took up space amidships. The trim would be affected by the distribution of fuel and fresh water, but there appeared to be no problems in removing the propelling machinery away from the centre of the ship.

The removal of all hatches and other obstructions made it easier to plan the public rooms and accommodation, and to introduce a large proportion of centreline cabins in the increased space. These cabins would be equipped with air conditioning, which would be attractive in comparison with the normal ship-side cabin. *Northern Star* took advantage of the experience gained in the operation of *Southern Cross*, which was regarded as revolutionary when she was introduced into service in 1955.

With the introduction of the *Transvaal Castle* in 1962, the Union Castle Line also recognised the problem of mixing cargo and passengers in the same vessel. The chairman, Sir Nicholas Cayzer, outlined the difficulty and expense caused by the time taken to load and discharge cargo while the passenger accommodation was idle. He felt that, 'for this reason the *Transvaal Castle* may well turn out to be the last, or nearly the last, of a long and proud line of ships. If that is so, it can truthfully be said that she concludes a chapter with a flourish.'

Transvaal Castle was designed as a 'Hotel-Class' ship to end the practice of having three sets of public rooms, three restaurants, three deck spaces and three staffs of stewards, with each segregated from the others. Sir Nicholas claimed that she was designed and built with an eye to the future. The old perception that there are two types of passenger, 'one clad in white tie and tails, and the other in shirt sleeves and braces no longer applies to our customers'. *Transvaal Castle* – with fares to Cape Town ranging from £700 for a luxury suite for two, to £120 for a berth in a shared inside cabin – was correctly described as an all-class ship rather than a one-class vessel. Like a hotel, passengers were able to choose accommodation ranging from a suite to a four-berth cabin, but all had the run of the ship, with its deck space, public rooms, cinema, swimming pool and other facilities. Sir Nicholas felt that 'the passenger ships have future, but they must be the right ships in the right place at the right time'.

The Union Castle Line had pioneered the use of one-class ships when they introduced the *Bloemfontein Castle* in 1950. She was followed by *Rhodesia Castle*, *Kenya Castle* and *Braemar Castle*, and passengers were able to use all of the public rooms and deck space. A large proportion of the cabins was within the cabin-class range of fares, but certain one- and two-

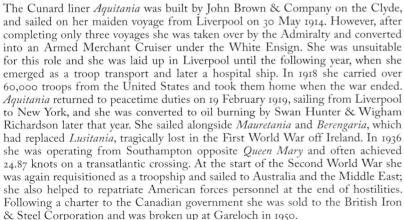

The Cunard liner *Aquitania* was built by John Brown & Company on the Clyde, and sailed on her maiden voyage from Liverpool on 30 May 1914. However, after completing only three voyages she was taken over by the Admiralty and converted into an Armed Merchant Cruiser under the White Ensign. She was unsuitable for this role and she was laid up in Liverpool until the following year, when she emerged as a troop transport and later a hospital ship. In 1918 she carried over 60,000 troops from the United States and took them home when the war ended. *Aquitania* returned to peacetime duties on 19 February 1919, sailing from Liverpool to New York, and she was converted to oil burning by Swan Hunter & Wigham Richardson later that year. She sailed alongside *Mauretania* and *Berengaria*, which had replaced *Lusitania*, tragically lost in the First World War off Ireland. In 1936 she was operating from Southampton opposite *Queen Mary* and often achieved 24.87 knots on a transatlantic crossing. At the start of the Second World War she was again requisitioned as a troopship and sailed to Australia and the Middle East; she also helped to repatriate American forces personnel at the end of hostilities. Following a charter to the Canadian government she was sold to the British Iron & Steel Corporation and was broken up at Gareloch in 1950.

Britannic was built by Harland & Wolff at Belfast. She was launched on 6 August 1929 and sailed on her maiden voyage from Liverpool to New York on 28 June 1930. The Cunard Line and White Star amalgamated on 10 May 1934, becoming Cunard-White Star, and *Britannic* made her first voyage from London to New York on 19 April 1935. She was requisitioned by the Admiralty on 29 August 1939 and operated as a troopship, being attacked by enemy aircraft in the Red Sea in October 1940 and by German U-boats in the Atlantic. She survived the hostilities and returned to the Liverpool–New York service on 22 May 1948. In June 1950 she collided with the American vessel *Pioneer Land* in New York harbour. Each winter she cruised in the Mediterranean and completed several world cruises with *Caronia*. She suffered a broken crankshaft in 1960 and was laid up briefly in New York. On 25 November 1960 she sailed on her last voyage from New York to Liverpool, as the last vessel to sail the North Atlantic in the colours of the White Star Line. *Britannic* was sold to ship-breakers at Inverkeithing and sailed from Liverpool on 16 December 1960 to be broken up by T. W. Ward.

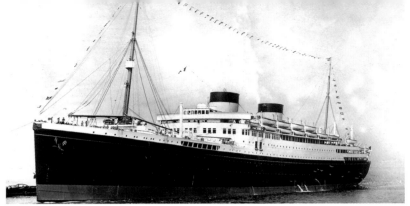

Oronsay was launched on 30 June 1950 by Vickers Armstrong at Barrow. She was similar to *Orcades*, and while under construction she suffered a serious fire at the fitting-out berth which took three days to extinguish. The blaze occurred in her number two hold, where it was confined. Her maiden voyage was delayed for two months because of this fire. She cost £4 million to build and sailed on her maiden voyage to Australia on 16 May 1951. She was the first Orient liner to be transferred to P&O ownership in 1964 and was later painted white. *Oronsay* became a popular vessel when she cruised in Australian waters at the end of her career, and was broken up in 1975.

The White Star liner *Georgic* sailed on her maiden voyage from Liverpool to New York on 25 June 1932. In 1933 she replaced *Olympic* during her overhaul on the Liverpool–New York service, and was transferred to the London–New York route in 1935. She returned to the Liverpool service in 1939, making five round voyages before she was requisitioned by the Admiralty as a troopship. She carried troops to Norway, France and then to the Middle East via Cape Town. On 22 May 1941 she left the Clyde for Port Tewfik, where she arrived on 7 July. While at anchor she was bombed and set on fire, and following an explosion she was beached. After an inspection it was decided to salvage the vessel. The pumps were used to clear the water from her hull, and she was towed to Port Sudan by *Clan Campbell* and the *City of Sydney*, which took thirteen days. The tug HMS *St Sampson* towed her to Karachi, and after inspection she was dry-docked at Bombay and loaded with ballast for the return journey to the United Kingdom. *Georgic* left Bombay on 20 January 1943 and arrived at Liverpool on 1 March, then proceeded to Belfast. On 16 December 1944 she was handed back to Cunard-White Star, who would manage her for the Ministry of Transport. The following year she carried out trooping duties to Italy, the Middle East and India, and repatriated over 5,000 Italian prisoners of war in 1946. She was refitted on the Tyne in 1948 and used for the emigrant service to Australia and New Zealand. However, on her first voyage from Liverpool to Fremantle, Melbourne and Sydney, with 1,200 people on board, a rope wrapped around the propeller and she had to enter the dock system for repairs. In 1950 she was chartered back to the Cunard Line for the Liverpool–New York service, and the Southampton–New York service, and the charter was repeated for the following four years. This was followed by further trooping duties, and on arrival at Liverpool on 16 April 1955 she was offered for sale. A charter by the Australian government followed, and on completion she was laid up in December that year at Kames Bay on the Clyde. She arrived at Faslane on 1 February the following year to be broken up.

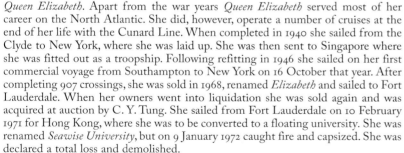

Queen Elizabeth. Apart from the war years *Queen Elizabeth* served most of her career on the North Atlantic. She did, however, operate a number of cruises at the end of her life with the Cunard Line. When completed in 1940 she sailed from the Clyde to New York, where she was laid up. She was then sent to Singapore where she was fitted out as a troopship. Following refitting in 1946 she sailed on her first commercial voyage from Southampton to New York on 16 October that year. After completing 907 crossings, she was sold in 1968, renamed *Elizabeth* and sailed to Fort Lauderdale. When her owners went into liquidation she was sold again and was acquired at auction by C. Y. Tung. She sailed from Fort Lauderdale on 10 February 1971 for Hong Kong, where she was to be converted to a floating university. She was renamed *Seawise University*, but on 9 January 1972 caught fire and capsized. She was declared a total loss and demolished.

Kenya Castle was built in 1952 by Harland & Wolff at Belfast, and she left on her maiden voyage, on the 'Round Africa' service on 4 April 1952. In 1959 her funnel was heightened and a dome was fitted to the top. She arrived at the River Fal on 22 April 1967 to be laid up following a relatively short career with the Union Castle Line. In October that year she was purchased by Chandris Lines and renamed *Amerikanis*. Following conversion to a cruising vessel at Piraeus she sailed on her first voyage to New York on 8 August 1968. As *Amerikanis* she cruised out of New York. Chandris Line was founded in 1960 to operate passenger liners between Greece and Australia. It traded under the names Greek Australian Line, National Greek Australian Line and Europe-Australia Line. The line merged with Chandris Cruises in 1974 to concentrate on cruising operations. Fantasy Cruises were acquired in 1985, becoming Chandris Fantasy Cruises, and Celebrity Cruises was founded in 1988; the name Chandris Lines ceased operations in 1996.

Queen Elizabeth 2 was built by John Brown & Company on the Clyde and was launched by Her Majesty Queen Elizabeth on 20 September 1967. She was employed on transatlantic crossings and also undertook cruises. In 1982 she participated in the Falklands Conflict and carried over 3,000 troops to the South Atlantic. She was converted from steam to diesel power in 1986/87, and the passenger accommodation was refurbished. When the Line was purchased by the Carnival Corporation in 1999, the QE2 received a $30 million refurbishment. She was acquired by Nakheel on 27 November 2008 and was laid up at Port Rashid in 2011. She was handed over to Nakheel at Dubai, and it is proposed that she is to be used as a hotel, restaurant and entertainment complex.

Canadian Pacific Steamships' map of Canada.

Braemar Castle was built in 1952 by Harland & Wolff, and was a sister ship of *Kenya Castle*. She also operated on the company's 'Round Africa' service. Her funnel was also heightened and a dome fitted in 1959, and she was employed cruising in 1965. However, she was withdrawn from service and arrived at Faslane on 6 January 1966 to be broken up.

bedded rooms, some with private bath or private shower, were let at higher rates. The lowest grade was within the tourist-class rates.

In the late 1950s, Cunard's Queens were reaching the end of their commercial life, and the company was looking at the type of vessel that would be required to replace them. The *United States* had taken the Blue Riband award, and France was introducing a new superliner to the North Atlantic route. The financing of a replacement liner was discussed in Parliament in 1959, and preliminary plans were drawn up to establish the costings for the project. The initial discussions centred on the plan to construct two 80,000-ton vessels with a speed of around 30 knots at a cost of £30 million for each ship. The government looked at the proposals and decided that it could not support the use of public money for this purpose.

In 1960 Cunard paid £8.5 million for Eagle Airways, as they were interested in operating on the routes between the United Kingdom and New York via Bermuda. They also negotiated a partnership with BOAC, which allowed the two companies to work together.

A government committee proposed a subsidy of £18 million on the basis of a one-ship solution to the problem of replacing the Queens, but Cunard were insisting that two ships were required to maintain their transatlantic service. Invitations to tender were issued in March 1961, and the project was known as 'Q3'. John Brown & Company, Fairfield's on the Clyde, Cammell Laird, Harland & Wolff and a joint tender by Vickers and Swan Hunter were invited to apply for the building of the vessel. It was announced at the time that Cunard Eagle Airways was not making a profit, and this led to the view of many that the project should be cancelled. Passenger numbers on the Queens were lower again, and in 1963 it was announced that both ships would undertake a series of cruises in-between their normal Atlantic duties.

Queen Elizabeth was equipped with a lido and outdoor swimming pool, and partial air conditioning was installed. In practice the idea was not a success, as the vessels were not suitable for cruise work, because of their size and lack of appropriate facilities. However, the North Atlantic Shipping Bill was passed by Parliament in June 1961, allowing Cunard to go ahead with the 'Q3' project. Three months later, Cunard announced that it was not ready to proceed on such an important order, and that it was looking at another alternative, 'Q4'.

It became clear that the 'Q4' project involved a vessel that would have a dual role, providing the North Atlantic service in the summer, and cruising in the winter months. Consequently, the design would have to be radically different to the original 'Q3', and that of the *United States* and her French competitor, the *France*.

Sir John Brocklebank, chairman of the Cunard Steam Ship Company, stated in 1961 that

the plan to build a 75,000 ton express passenger ship as a replacement for the *Queen Mary* originated over two years ago. Since then the North Atlantic passenger trade had become considerably less remunerative, particularly in the second half of the year. This fall in profits has been accentuated by disturbances in the international situation.

Other factors that were having an adverse effect upon Cunard's earnings were the tendency of the potential first-class passenger across the North Atlantic to use air travel to an increasing extent, and the fact that operating costs, such as ship management, repairs and wages, continued to increase but could not be offset by raising fares, in view of intense competition from air travel.

The directors of Cunard said that they regretted to announce that in these circumstances the company would postpone for the time being the decision to place an order for a ship as a replacement for the *Queen Mary*. They said that the decision had been made with regret, and that it had been conveyed to the government and to the shipbuilders who submitted tenders. The full effect of the increasingly adverse operating results on the North Atlantic had only just become apparent, and in consequence the Cunard Board decided on a complete reassessment of their services. It was agreed that the extent of the company's investment in air transport and its relation with Cunard's shipping interests would be subject to close examination, and they did not expect this to be completed before the second quarter of 1962.

The chairman stated that there were other reasons for the decision to postpone, including a change in the composition of the traffic, as well as the quantity; the fall in 1961 being almost entirely in first-class traffic; and also Cunard's thoughts on the size of ship that could be built with 'advanced techniques'. However, it appears that Cunard were encouraged by the Swan Hunter/Vickers Armstrong tender being under £30 million, even allowing for reasonable escalation for increased costs during construction.

Cunard had carried 10 per cent fewer passengers than the previous year, amounting to around 100,000 passengers. They also made a loss on their investment in Cunard Eagle Airways Limited and in their subsidiary, Thos. & Jno. Brocklebank. However, the two Queens continued to operate profitably. It was widely speculated that the proposals for a new ship centred on the idea of a 55,000/60,000-ton vessel, costing some £20–£22 million. The company were basing their plans on the fact that there would always be a number of people who prefered to cross the Atlantic by sea than by air, and corresponding profits would be made by 'the best ships available to carry them provided that fleets are so organised that they can provide more berths in summer than in winter'.

In 1963 *Caronia* was again fully employed cruising, but unfortunately the World and Spring Cruises were not as successful as hoped, due to the Cuba crisis during the previous autumn. The cruise market improved for the latter half of the year, and this continued into 1964 with good support for the World and other long cruises. *Mauretania* repeated her normal cruise programme from New York to the West Indies, followed by a Mediterranean cruise. She was scheduled for a further four voyages to the West Indies during the autumn. *Queen Elizabeth* made three cruises to Nassau in the early part of the year, followed by a further two cruises to Nassau from New York over the Thanksgiving holiday, and in these five voyages she carried over 5,100 passengers.

Cruising from the United Kingdom was resumed by Cunard in 1963, for the first time since the Second World War, and *Queen Mary* made two cruises over Christmas and the New Year, followed by a third cruise at Easter 1964. The conversion of *Franconia* and *Carmania*, which took place in the early part of 1963, enabled Cunard to employ the two ships in cruising from American ports, and a new venture that proved to be popular was the inauguration of the cruise service out of Port Everglades to the West Indies with *Carmania*, while her sister ship *Franconia* cruised to the Caribbean from New York. During the winter of 1963/4 no less than six of Cunard's eight passenger ships were engaged in cruising from United States and British ports.

The *Queen Elizabeth* made a successful maiden cruise from New York to the Mediterranean, of twenty-five days' duration, in 1964, in addition to five cruises to Nassau. For the first time, *Queen Elizabeth* operated a Christmas cruise to Nassau from New York that attracted capacity carrying. *Queen Mary* and *Mauretania* operated cruises out of the United Kingdom to the Atlantic Isles and the Mediterranean, together with a cruise to the West Indies by *Mauretania*. Cunard operated thirty-seven cruises from American ports and the United Kingdom in 1964, as compared to twenty-one in 1963.

The order for the new vessel was finally placed with John Brown on the Clyde by Cunard on 30 December 1964, and she was launched as *Queen Elizabeth 2* by Her Majesty Queen Elizabeth on 20 September 1967. Following some initial problems on her trials, she sailed on her maiden voyage from Southampton to New York on 2 May 1969, and thus began the career of one of Britain's most famous and successful ocean liners.

Carinthia in the St Lawrence. She was the third sister in the *Saxonia* class to enter service, and was built on the Clyde by John Brown & Co. Ltd. She sailed on her maiden voyage from Liverpool to Quebec and Montreal on 27 June 1956, and was chartered by the Canadian government in 1960 as a troopship for NATO. On 13 October 1967 she made the last passenger sailing for the Cunard Line from Liverpool to Montreal, and returned to Southampton, where she was laid up. She was sold to the Sitmar Line in 1968 and was initially renamed *Fairland* for their Southampton–New Zealand route, but continued to be laid up at Southampton. She finally sailed to Trieste in January 1970; Sitmar completed a restyling of the vessel during 1970–71, and she entered service in the American cruise market in 1972 as *Fairsea*. She accommodated 910 first-class passengers, and her tonnage was increased to 21,916 tons. When Sitmar was purchased by P&O in 1988 she was renamed *Fair Princess*, and *China Seas Discovery* in 2000, when she was owned by Emerald Cruises. She was broken up at Alang, where she arrived on 18 November 2005.

Empress of Britain Sports Deck.

The Canadian Pacific Railway Company's passenger vessels *Empress of Britain* and *Empress of Canada* at their berth in Gladstone Dock. *Empress of Britain* was built by the Fairfield Ship Building & Engineering Company in 1956 for the Canadian service from Liverpool, and for cruising during the winter months. She was chartered to the Travel Savings Association in 1963, and sold to the Greek Line the following year, becoming *Queen Anna Maria*. She was employed on their transatlantic service until 1975, when she was laid up at Piraeus. She was then sold to the Carnival Cruise Line and renamed *Carnivale*, *Fiesta Marina* and *Olympic* in 1994, *Topaz* in 1997 and then chartered as the Peace Boat until 2008. Following a period laid up at Singapore she was broken up at Alang later that year. *Empress of Canada* operated for Canadian Pacific until 1972 when she was sold to Carnival Cruise Line and renamed *Mardi Gras*, *Olympic* in 1993, *Star of Texas* in 1994 and *Apollon* in 1996. She was broken up in 2004.

Galleon Bar on the *Cunard Adventurer*.

Cunard Adventurer suffered an engine room failure on her delivery voyage, and drifted for four hours in the Bay of Biscay. She eventually managed to get to Lisbon, where her mechanical problems were resolved and she was able to continue her journey. She operated for the Cunard Line until 1977, when she was sold to the Norwegian Cruise Line and renamed *Sunward II*, became *Triton* in 1991 for the Epirotiki Line and Royal Olympic Cruises, and *Coral*, owned by Louis Cruises in 2004. It was announced that she was to be renamed *Louis Rhea* in 2014 but she was then sold to be broken up at Alang, and renamed *Cora*.

Cunard Princess. She was launched as *Cunard Conquest*, and christened by Princess Grace of Monaco at New York, on 29 March 1977, as *Cunard Princess*. She sailed on 2 April to Bermuda to begin her weekly summer cruises, and winter cruises were from Florida to San Juan. In 1986 *Cunard Princess* was employed on Panama Canal cruises from New York. Together with *Cunard Countess* she was transferred to Cunard Crown Cruises, but in 1995 she was operating as *Rhapsody* on charter to StarLauro Cruises. She was later purchased by them and registered in Panama. The company became Mediterranean Shipping Cruises, later MSC Cruises. *Rhapsody* was sold to Mano Maritime in 2009 and renamed *Golden Iris*, operating on cruises from Haifa to Cyprus, the Greek Islands, Montenegro, Italy and Croatia.

When her keel was laid in 1937 *Mauretania* became the largest liner to be built in England and was the first passenger liner to be constructed for the Cunard-White Star Line. She was built without any government subsidy and was designed to relieve the *Queen Mary* when required. She was launched at the yard of Cammell Laird on 28 July 1938 from slipway number 6, and the following March she sailed out of the Mersey on her acceptance trials, achieving an average speed of 22 knots.

Her maiden voyage took place on 17 June 1939, when large crowds on both sides of the Mersey saw her sail from the Pier Head to New York. In August that year she was transferred to the London–New York service and became the largest vessel to use the King George V dock. On 14 September she made a voyage from Southampton to New York, returning to Liverpool, and after another round trip she sailed to New York, where she was laid up on 16 December 1939.

In March 1940 she became a troopship and sailed from New York to Sydney via the Panama Canal and Honolulu for conversion. On 5 May she sailed from Sydney to the Clyde with over 2,000 troops. Over the period of the Second World War *Mauretania* made forty-eight trooping voyages, covering 540,000 miles, and carried over 355,000 troops.

She arrived back on the Mersey on 2 August 1946 to be converted back to a passenger liner at Gladstone Dock, Liverpool, by her builders. On 18 April the following year, when the work was completed, she left Liverpool on a 2½-day short cruise, but because of bad weather she was unable to return until five days later. However, on 26 April she restarted the Liverpool–New York service and later transferred to Southampton.

In 1957 she was fitted with air conditioning during her overhaul, so she was able to undertake a programme of cruises including around-the-world voyages. During her winter overhaul in 1962 she was painted in 'Caronia' green, and the following year she was placed on the New York–Cannes–Genoa–Naples service. Her final sailing on this service was on 15 September 1965, and she returned to Southampton where she was sold to be broken up. She arrived at Inverkeithing on 23 November to be scrapped by Thos W. Ward.

Iberia was built for the P&O Line in 1954 by Harland & Wolff at Belfast. She sailed on her maiden voyage from London to Bombay, Colombo, Melbourne and Sydney on 28 September 1954. On 27 March 1956 she was badly damaged in a collision with the tanker *Stanvac Pretoria* near Colombo. During her overhaul in 1961 she was fitted with full air conditioning and stabilisers. Following her last voyage to Australia in 1972, she was employed on cruising duties but was sold early the following year and broken up at Kaohsiung.

Arcadia was launched on 14 May 1953 for P&O at the yard of John Brown & Co. Ltd on the Clyde. She sailed on her maiden voyage to Australia on 22 February the following year. *Arcadia* was also fitted with full air conditioning in 1959 and was then placed on the trans-Pacific route. She operated cruises from the west coast of America to Alaska and Mexico during 1974, and offered cruises from Australia, replacing *Himalaya* the following year. *Arcadia* was broken up at Kaohsiung in 1979.

Spirit of London was built for the P&O Line and was the first P&O passenger vessel to be built exclusively for cruising. She was built in Italy by C. N. del Tirreno & Riuniti, Riva Trigosa, and was launched on 29 April 1972. P&O took over the contract for the vessel from the Norwegian Klosters Rederi, and she sailed on her maiden voyage from Southampton to San Juan on 11 November 1972. She was renamed *Sun Princess* in 1974, and *Starship Majestic* and *Southern Cross* in 1995. She became *Flamenco* when owned by Festival Cruises in 1997, *Elysian Flamenco* in 2004, *New Flamenco* in 2005.

Himalaya was built for the P&O Line by Vickers Armstrong at Barrow in 1949 for the Tilbury–Australia service. In 1958 she was placed on the trans-Pacific service and was converted to a one-class vessel in 1963, following the withdrawal of the last 'Strath' class vessel. In 1974 she was sold to be broken up.

Southern Cross sails from Liverpool on a cruise in 1972.

Launch of P&O's *Spirit of London* on 11 May 1972.

Andes was another product of Harland & Wolff at Belfast, and was launched on 7 March 1939. She was due to make her maiden voyage on the 100th anniversary of the Royal Mail Lines but was ordered to sail to Liverpool, where she was converted to a troopship. In May 1945 she carried the Norwegian government back to Oslo, and was returned to her builders to be prepared for peacetime service, sailing on 22 January 1948 on her first commercial voyage to South America. In 1959 she was converted to a one-class vessel and sailed on her first cruise in June the following year. *Andes* was advertised as being 'not just another passenger liner that converts to cruising for a few months each year. She is a 27,000 ton ship with a crew of 460 men and women, devoted entirely to cruising, indeed dedicated to make sure that your cruise is the most memorable holiday of your life.' She boasted having 40,000 square feet of open deck, an outdoor swimming pool, a golf net for practising, a 250-seat air-conditioned cinema, bridge in the Warwick Room, dancing, bingo and deck games. The 1970 brochure claimed that 'you can do and get pretty well anything you want in Andes, within the limits of decency, that is!' She was a popular and successful cruise ship and survived until 1971, when she was sold and broken up at Ghent.

Reina del Mar sails on a Travel Savings Association Cruise.

Dept. of Industry

UK Owned & Registered Fleet (Trading Ships 500 grt & over) 31st March 1982
(30th June 1981 figures in brackets)

Ship Type	No.	dwt (000)
Passenger/Cargo	92 (99)	169 (177)
Cellular Container	68 (72)	1462 (1500)
Other Cargo Liner	156 (191)	1863 (2196)
Total Liner	316 (362)	3494 (3873)
Bulk Carrier	290 (309)	7495 (7818)
Other Tramp	45 (49)	220 (258)
Total Tramp	335 (358)	7715 (8076)
Tanker	327 (362)	18385 (21293)
Total All Ships	978 (1082)	29593 (33241)

Pacific Princess was built in 1971 by Rheinstahl Nordseewerke at Emden with accommodation for 650 passengers in one class. She was built as *Sea Venture* for Norwegian Cruise Ships A/S, Oslo. It was reported that the builders lost £2 million on the order for *Sea Venture* and her sister, and a third vessel was cancelled. She was introduced on the New York–Bermuda route until the line was purchased by P&O in 1974. Renamed *Pacific Princess*, she was placed on the Pacific cruise service from Los Angeles in 1975. She was featured in the television series *The Love Boat* from 1976 to 1987. In 2002 she was operating for Pullmantur Cruises in the Caribbean, and also by Quail Cruises. Following a dispute over an unpaid repair bill, an attempt was made to sell the vessel at auction in 2010 and 2011. She arrived at Aliaga on 6 August 2013 to be broken up.

UK Owned & Registered Fleet.

Uganda was built by Barclay, Curle, for the British India Lines service from London to East Africa. She sailed on her maiden voyage on 2 August 1951 from London to Beira, and was painted with an all-white hull in 1955. The East African service was withdrawn in 1966 and *Uganda* was converted to an educational cruise ship at Howaldswerke at Hamburg in 1967. She sailed on her first cruise on 27 February 1968, and in 1972 ownership was transferred to the P&O Line. She was taken over by the British government on 10 April 1982 and used as a hospital ship in the Falkland Islands. She briefly resumed cruises later that year but was chartered to the government again in 1983 for use between Ascension Island and the Falklands. She returned to the United Kingdom in 1985 and was laid up and sold to the ship-breakers in 1986. She was renamed *Triton* for the delivery voyage to Kaohsiung, where she arrived on 15 July. She had been sold to An Hsiung Iron & Steel Company at Kaohsiung and was registered in the ownership of Triton Shipping Company, Barbados, for the voyage to the breakers, then was anchored outside the harbour while negotiations took place as to a possible resale. However, she was driven aground by typhoon Wayne on 22 August and heeled over onto her side, demolished as she lay.

Department of Industry.

	December 1975		December 1980		June 1985	
	No.	mn.dwt.	No.	mn.dwt.	No.	mn.dwt.
TANKERS	454	30.0	381	23.3	214	9.8
DRY BULK CARRIERS	546	14.3	374	8.1	215	4.3
PASSENGER FERRIES/ CRUISE SHIPS	112	0.2	100	0.2	83	0.2
CELLULAR CONTAINER SHIPS	89	1.3	71	1.5	52	1.4
CARGO LINERS	413	4.1	215	2.5	83	1.0
TOTAL	1,614	50.0	1,141	35.6	647	16.6

P&O's *Oriana* in the Solent. She was built in 1960 by Vickers Armstrong at Barrow-in-Furness, and carried members of the Association of British Travel Agents on their convention on her maiden voyage. She sailed on her first voyage to Australia from Southampton, and returned via Sydney, Auckland, Vancouver and San Francisco. *Oriana* operated as a cruise ship from 1973, when she was converted to a one-class vessel, and was based in Australian waters between 1981 and 1986. The ship was laid up at Sydney for a short time before she was sold to become a floating hotel at Osaka. From 1987 she operated as a floating museum at Beppu Oita and was sold to become a floating attraction in Shanghai in 1995. However, she was moved to Dalian in 2002, where she was severely damaged by a storm in 2004 and was broken up by ship-breakers the following year.

Canberra was launched at the yard of Harland & Wolff on 16 March 1960 by Dame Pattie Menzies, wife of the then prime minister of Australia. She sailed on her maiden voyage from Southampton to Colombo, Melbourne and Sydney on 2 June the following year. In 1974 she was converted to carry out full-time cruising duties. She was requisitioned by the Ministry of Defence as a troopship in 1982, following the Argentine invasion of the Falkland Islands. *Canberra* sailed from Southampton on 9 April for the South Atlantic, and was quickly nicknamed the 'Great White Whale' when transporting members of the Parachute Regiment and Royal Marines to the islands. On arrival she was anchored in San Carlos Water, where she was vulnerable to air attacks by Argentine aircraft. However, she was never hit and later moved to South Georgia, where 3,000 troops were transferred from *Queen Elizabeth 2*; they were later landed at San Carlos. At the end of hostilities she returned to Southampton, where she arrived on 11 July. Following an extensive overhaul she returned to cruise-ship operation and was very popular with her regular clientele. She survived until 1997, when she was sold and broken up on Gadani Beach in Pakistan.

Vistafjord was built for the Norwegian America Line by Swan Hunter on the Tyne in 1973. She was sold to the Cunard Line in 1973 and marketed by them under her original name until 1999, when she became *Caronia*. She was launched on 15 May 1972 and delivered to her owners exactly one year later on 15 May 1973; she holds the distinction of being the last cruise ship to have been built in the United Kingdom. Her maiden voyage took place on 22 May 1973, when she sailed from Oslo to New York and was then employed cruising from New York to the Bahamas. She was purchased by the Cunard Line in 1983 and retained her original name and colours, but was given a Cunard-colours funnel. On 10 December 1999 she was renamed *Caronia* at Liverpool Landing Stage. *Caronia* was purchased by Saga Cruises in 2004, and was sent to Valetta where she was given a £17-million refit and renamed *Saga Ruby*, joining her sister *Sagafjord*, which had become *Saga Rose*. She completed her final cruise early in 2014 and was dry-docked at Gibraltar prior to sailing to Burma, where she was converted to a floating hotel.

Above: Taras Shevchenko and her near sisters *Aleksandr Pushkin*, *Shota Rustaveli*, *Ivan Franko* and *Mikhail Lermontov* were built between 1963 and 1972 by VEB Mathias-Thesen Werft. She operated for the Black Sea Shipping Company between 1967 and 1995, Blasco UK from 1995 to 1997, and Ocean Agencies from 1997 to 2004. She was renamed *Tara* and broken up in India in 2005.

Right: Sea Goddess II.

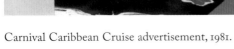

Carnival Caribbean Cruise advertisement, 1981.

Sea Goddess I.

Hebridean Princess.

P&O's *Adonia* berthed at the Liverpool Cruise Terminal on an Around Britain cruise.

Top right: *Royal Princess* was built at Helsinki in 1984 for Princess Cruises' United States operations. She was transferred to P&O in 2005, becoming *Artemis*, and was based in Southampton offering cruises to the British market. She was sold to Phoenix-Reisen in 2011 and renamed *Artania*.

Bottom right: Cruise & Maritime Voyages' *Ocean Countess*, leaving Liverpool on a cruise to the Mediterranean.

Empress of Canada was the final vessel in the trio of new Canadian Pacific liners introduced in the 1950s and 1960s for the Liverpool–Canada service via Greenock. She was the largest ship built for the route, and was air conditioned throughout, even on the glass-enclosed promenade decks. *Empress of Canada* was conceived and designed as a modern cargo-passenger liner for the North Atlantic service and for winter cruising in tropical climes.

The fact that she would be engaged in two trades meant that a compromise had to be made with her design, as the first consideration was the provision of a staple 'bread and butter' liner service between Britain and Canada, and during the winter months she would leave the well-travelled Atlantic route and begin her cruising schedule. Special attention was made to converting her from her two-class service to a single class for cruising. Public rooms covered a greater total area than in any other post-war Canadian Pacific liner, and large, unobstructed areas of open deck space were provided.

Accommodation ladders and landing platforms were specially constructed, and four launches supplied, adapted for embarking seventy passengers at a time at intermediate ports. When on cruise service, *Empress of Canada* would carry 750 one-class passengers, and on the North Atlantic run 1,048 passengers would be carried, 192 first class and 856 tourist. She was designed with 112 first-class staterooms and 293 tourist-class staterooms. Several communication doors were arranged to allow two staterooms to form a single unit, and others were equipped with settee-type beds for conversion to sitting rooms during the day.

At the planning stage various alternatives were considered for the design of *Empress of Canada* as a dual-purpose vessel. The alternatives looked at were having the machinery aft, amidships with centreline casings, and amidships with split casings. All aspects were carefully considered, including the idea of a funnel-less profile, but the company decided to adhere to the pattern previously established.

The popularity of the seven-day North Atlantic voyage was enhanced by the fact that two days were spent in the sheltered estuary of the St Lawrence. This 1,000-mile-long route, with rocky coasts, hills, towns, cities and forests, made it an unusual setting for an ocean voyage. Six hours out from Montreal, chimneys of the famous paper mills of the Three Rivers could be seen, and the ship slid under Quebec Bridge and past Quebec City. The route then took the ship through the narrow strait of Belle Isle or via Cape Race, Newfoundland. It is easy to see why many passengers regarded the North Atlantic transit as an enjoyable cruise.

The Boeing 747 aircraft's first flight took place on 9 February 1970, and its introduction forever changed the way people travelled around the world. The aircraft was a major factor in the demise of passenger liner services in the 1960s and 1970s. Together with the development of containerisation, the Boeing 747 brought about a dramatic change in the pattern of passenger and cargo services provided by shipping operators. It was two and a half times larger than the Boeing 707, and operated as a passenger- or a freight-carrying aircraft. The 747-400 has a range of 7,260 nautical miles and can carry up to 660 passengers.

Air travel became increasingly popular in the 1960s with the introduction of the Boeing 707 and Douglas DC-8. It was Pan American Airways who envisaged an aircraft twice the size of these, and Boeing were asked to come up with a design for this mammoth carrier. It was thought at the time that this design may have a short shelf life as it would soon be superseded by supersonic aircraft. It was important that the new aircraft could be easily adapted to carry freight when required. The contract for the first 747 was signed by Pan American and Boeing in April 1966, and consequently Pan Am had a greater influence in the design of the new aircraft.

It was fitted with a revolutionary high-bypass turbofan engine, which was developed by Boeing, Pan American and Pratt & Whitney. The aircraft was built at a new plant near Seattle, and the first flight took place on 9 February 1969, with test pilots Jack Waddell and Brian Wygle in command. Following a display at the Paris Air Show in 1969, the 747 received its FAA airworthiness certificate in December that year. It entered service on 22 January 1970 on Pan American's New York–London service. This was followed by orders received from all of the major airlines. However, during the recession of the early 1970s Boeing sold few of the aircraft, and some airlines converted them to freight carriers and used smaller passenger aircraft. However, as economic conditions improved, orders for the aircraft resumed, and it was developed and improved by the manufacturer.

As the advantages of air travel became apparent to the traveller, it was becoming clear to the shipping lines that the airlines were making considerable inroads into their passenger traffic. Although *Mauretania* carried out cruises as well as her transatlantic duties it was decided that she would be painted 'Caronia' green in 1962, and her cruise programme was increased. *Saxonia* and *Ivernia* were sent back to their builders for a major refit, which included the construction of a lido deck and swimming pool, and the installation of air conditioning. They emerged as *Carmania* and *Franconia* and were given the dual role of transatlantic liners in the summer and cruising vessels during the winter months. *Sylvania* and *Carinthia* were slightly modified and upgraded, and this was followed by work carried out on the *Queen Elizabeth* to allow her to take on cruising duties.

Cunard introduced its Fly and Cruise holidays in February 1967; *Sylvania* was based at Gibraltar for a series of Mediterranean cruises and her sister *Carmania* was similarly employed the following year. The British currency restrictions of the 1960s were advantageous to the cruise operators as there was a limit of £50 on the amount of currency or traveller's cheques that holidaymakers could take out of the country. However, as sterling was used on the cruise ships, passengers only needed to use their allowance at ports of call on the cruise.

In 1969 the American Overseas National Airways Incorporated placed an order with the Rotterdamsche Droogdok Maatschappij NV (Rotterdam Drydock Co. Ltd) for the construction of a 750-passenger cruise liner with options for two similar vessels. The Cunard Line acquired a 50 per cent interest and, when Overseas National Airways withdrew, Cunard took over sole responsibility for the project. The vessel had been built to the standards of the American Bureau of Shipping as it had been intended that the ship would operate under the Unites States flag. Consequently, the *Cunard Adventurer* became the first Cunard passenger vessel not to be classified by Lloyd's Register of Shipping. The name of the ship also departed from the Cunard tradition of naming (the name ending in 'ia'), which had previously only been changed by the introduction of *Queen Mary* and *Queen Elizabeth*.

Cunard Adventurer was given a Department of Trade and Industry certificate for 832 passengers, and complied with the safety standards and fire protection regulations laid down by the United States Public Health authorities and the United States Coast Guard. She sailed on her maiden voyage in November 1971 from Southampton to Lisbon, Madeira, Las Palmas, Antigua, Martinique, St Thomas and San Juan. She was then based at San Juan and cruised to St Thomas, St Lucia, Grenada, La Guaira and Curaçao.

Cunard and BOAC provided a holiday package from the United Kingdom, and also combined hotel/cruise holiday at Cunard Group hotels in St Lucia and Barbados. These were organised through Sunair Holidays Limited, of which Cunard acquired a 75 per cent shareholding in 1971. The second vessel was named *Cunard Ambassador* on 16 March 1972. She was a near sister of the *Cunard Adventurer*, and was also designed to operate short stage cruises with overnight passage between ports.

The final nail in the coffin for many British ships employed in cruising was the fourfold increase in fuel cost that took place in 1973–74. Many of the ships were relatively old, and they soon became uneconomic to operate. The

Saga Sapphire was built as *Europe* in 1981 for Hapag-Lloyd Cruises. She was sold to Star Cruises in 1999, and renamed *SuperStar Europe*, then *SuperStar Aires* the following year. Purchased by Pullmantur Cruises in 2004, she became *Holiday Dream* and was transferred to CDF Croisières de France in 2008 and renamed *Bleu de France*. She was purchased by Saga in 2012 and was sent to Fincantieri for an extensive refit, which included a complete overhaul of her engines and machinery, and adding new cabins.

Discovery was built as *Island Venture* for Flagship Cruises in 1972 and was sold, with her sister *Sea Venture*, to P&O Princess Cruises in 1974. *Island Venture* was renamed *Island Princess*, with *Sea Venture* becoming *Pacific Princess*. *Island Princess* was sold to Hyundai Merchant Marine in 1999 and renamed *Hyundai Pungak*, then became *Platinum* in 2001. From 2002 she has been operating as *Discovery* for Voyages of Discovery, part of the All Leisure Group, cruising out of several ports in the United Kingdom. She also operates in various parts of the world in the Northern Hemisphere winter months.

Cunard advertising poster of the 1920s.

Cunard advertising poster from the 2000s.

Oriana at San Francisco. She was built by Meyer Werft at Papenburg in Germany for P&O Cruises, and was named by Her Majesty Queen Elizabeth on 6 April 1995. She was owned by P&O Princess Cruises in 2000, and in 2003 the company merged with the Carnival Corporation. Following an extensive £12-million overhaul in 2006, she was reregistered in Bermuda, and a new restaurant was fitted; the Lords Tavern Bar was extended and her cabins were refurbished.

Aurora was also built by Meyer Werft at Papenburg for P&O Cruises, and was named by The Princess Royal, Princess Anne, on 27 April 2000. *Oriana* and *Aurora* were both designed and built for the British cruise market, and also to undertake world cruises each year. At the time of the attack on the World Trade Center at New York on 11 September 2001, *Aurora* was operating 80 miles away on a conference of IT personnel. Following the attacks *Aurora* was briefly protected by US Coastguard helicopters and was unable to return to her berth at Pier 53 in Manhattan. She was diverted to Boston, where her passengers were finally disembarked. Many of the people on board were in touch by phone with staff in Tower 1 and Tower 2, and would normally have been working at the World Trade Center.

Queen Victoria. The keel of *Queen Victoria* was laid on 12 May 2006, and the superstructure floated out in January the following year. She commenced her trials on 24 August 2007 and was named by Her Royal Highness the Duchess of Cornwall at Southampton; she sailed on her maiden cruise on 11 December that year. At 92,000 tons she is the second-largest vessel ever owned by Cunard. At the start of her first world cruise she sailed in tandem across the Atlantic with *Queen Elizabeth 2*, meeting *Queen Mary 2* in New York on 13 January 2008.

Queen Mary 2 in the Mersey. *Queen Mary 2* sailed from Southampton on her maiden voyage to Fort Lauderdale on 12 January 2004 carrying 2,620 passengers. She was the longest, widest and tallest passenger ship ever built, and was designed as an ocean liner and cruise ship.

On 23 February 2006, *Queen Mary 2* arrived at Long Beach and exchanged a salute with the original *Queen Mary*, which is berthed at the port. On her first world cruise, *Queen Mary 2* met *Queen Elizabeth 2* at Sydney on 20 February 2007. It was the first time that two Cunard Queens had been together in Sydney since the original *Queen Mary* and *Queen Elizabeth* had been there on trooping duties in 1941.

Empress of Australia was laid down as *Suffren* for the French Line, and launched as *De Grasse* on 23 February 1924, at the yard of Cammell Laird & Co. Ltd at Birkenhead. She was completed at St Nazaire, after being towed there following a strike at the builder's yard. In June 1940, she was taken over by the Germans at Bordeaux and used as an accommodation ship, and later as a depot ship for Italian submarines operating in the Atlantic. When the German forces withdrew from the port, she was sunk by them on 25 August 1944. She was raised the following year, and emerged from the shipyard with one funnel, taking her first post-war sailing from Le Havre to New York on 12 July 1947. In the early 1950s she was transferred to the West Indies service, and following the fire and sinking of the *Empress of Canada* in Gladstone Dock, Liverpool, she was purchased by Canadian Pacific in 1953. She was renamed *Empress of Australia* and took her first sailing from Liverpool to Quebec on 25 April that year. She was laid up at Liverpool in December 1955, and with the new *Empress of Britain* being delivered in April 1956 she was sold to Grimaldi-Siosa and renamed *Venezuela* for their Naples–La Guaira service. On 17 March 1962 she grounded off Cannes and was refloated the following month, but was declared uneconomic to repair and was broken up at La Spezia.

Empress of Canada was launched as *Duchess of Richmond* on 18 June 1928 and left on her maiden voyage, which was a cruise to the Canary Islands, on 26 January 1929. Early in 1935 she carried the Duke and Duchess of Kent on their honeymoon cruise, and was requisitioned by the Admiralty in 1940 as a troopship. At the end of the war she returned to service as *Empress of Canada* on the Liverpool–Quebec–Montreal route in the summer, cruising in the winter months. On 25 January 1953 she caught fire and capsized in Gladstone Dock, Liverpool, and a salvage operation commenced, which took until the following March to right the ship. She was taken to Gladstone Drydock and made watertight before she was towed to Italy and broken up. She left Liverpool on 1 September 1954.

Canadian Pacific advertisement.

Reina del Pacifico was built for the Pacific Steam Navigation Company by Harland & Wolff in 1931. She was delivered on 27 March and undertook a three-day North Sea shakedown cruise prior to sailing on her maiden voyage from Liverpool to La Rochelle–Vigo–Bermuda–Bahamas–Havana–Jamaica–Panama Canal–Guayaquil–Callao–Antofagasta–Valparaiso in 25½ days. In 1932 she offered a 'Round South America' cruise, which was repeated once a year until the end of the decade. On 9 November 1937, Britain's first Labour prime minister, James Ramsay MacDonald, died of heart failure while on board *Reina del Pacifico*. She was requisitioned as a troopship by the Admiralty in 1939, and carried troops to Norway, West Africa, Suez via Cape Town, South Africa and India. In 1943 she transported King Peter of Yugoslavia, and transported the United States First Division headquarters staff to Britain for the preparations for the Normandy landings. At the end of the war it was calculated that she had sailed over 350,000 miles and carried 150,000 personnel as a repatriation ship. In 1947 she was returned to her builders for a major overhaul and to be prepared for her return to commercial service. However, on 11 September that year she suffered a serious engine explosion in which twenty-eight people lost their lives after a piston overheated. In 1957 she went aground on Devil's Flat, Bermuda, and later that year she lost a propeller at Havana. *Reina del Pacifico* left Liverpool on her final voyage to South America on 27 April 1958, and was broken up by John Cashmore at Newport.

Above: 1950–51 Round voyages by regular passenger ships.

Right: Following the success of cruising in the years prior to the outbreak of the Second World War, and improvements in the economy, the opportunity to take a holiday on a ship was soon offered to prospective passengers. The holiday firm Dean & Dawson advertised a number of cruises on cargo ships and round voyages by regular passenger ships. Their 1950–51 brochure claimed that 'these pleasures are back again and you can think in practical terms of sea voyaging far away from English shores, study the wide choice of voyages and see yourself climbing the gangway to the gracious, spacious days of pre-war cruising'. Many of the cargo vessels that were built to replace those lost during the war were designed with accommodation for a small number of passengers, who had the full run of the ships, which were all modern vessels with up-to-date facilities and accommodation. Dean & Dawson also advertised 'voyages combining a long sea passage with extensive tours in distant parts of the Empire'. They offered round trips on cargo vessels and tankers where there was no regular schedule or itinerary. 'The friendly, self–contained community aboard quickly becomes adept at making its own entertainment. The good food and an appetite sharpened by the sea air add to the feeling of wellbeing. In no other way can complete idleness be indulged with such an easy conscience or do you so much in body and mind'.

Approx. duration	Route and main ports of call	Line Ship Gross Tonnage	Sailings from	Round Voyage Fare from
140 days	Round the World via N. America, Panama, Far East, Ceylon & Suez Canal	Ellerman Lines	U.K. port occasional	£500
130 days	Round the World via N. America, Panama, New Zealand, Australia & Suez Canal	Ellerman Lines	U.K. port occasional	£450
105 days	Via Suez & Colombo to Bangkok (Siam)	East Asiatic Line	Irregular	£333
90 days	Panama, California (Los Angeles, San Francisco) & British Columbia (Vancouver)	Holland-America Line "Dalerdijk" 10,820 tons (and others)	Rotterdam approx. monthly	£273 to £351 according to ship
90 days	Panama, California & British Columbia (Vancouver)	Royal Mail Lines	U.K. port approx. monthly	£356
72 days	Panama & West Coast of S. America to Valparaiso (Chile)	Pacific S.N. Co.	Liverpool approx. every 3 months	£206 plus amount for stay on board whilst at destination port
70 days	Panama, California and Vancouver	Furness Line	Liverpool occasionally	£286
70 days	Brazil (Rio de Janeiro), Uruguay (Montevideo), and Argentine (Buenos Aires)	S. American Saint Line "St. Thomas" 7,192 tons (and others)	U.K. port occasional	£176 or £238 according to ship, plus £1 daily whilst in destination port
56 days	West Africa (Dakar, Freetown, Accra, etc.)	Holland West Africa Line	U.K. ports occasional	£180
49-56 days	Greece, Turkey, Bulgaria & Rumania	Royal Netherlands S.S. Co.	Every fortnight	£101 10s.
49 days	Adriatic (Italy & Yugoslavia)	Royal Netherlands S.S. Co.	Every 3 weeks	£89 2s.
45-55 days	Egypt (Alexandria) & Lebanon (Beirut)	Euxine Line "Nefertiti" 2,280 tons (and others)	U.K. ports approx. twice monthly	£120
45-50 days	Cuba (Havana) Mexican & Gulf ports	Holland-America Line	Rotterdam or Antwerp approx. monthly	£157
42-49 days	Mexican Gulf, U.S.A. (New Orleans, Galveston, Houston, Mobile. etc.)	Ropner Line "Daleby" and "Deerpool" 4,800 tons	U.K. ports about monthly	£150
42-49 days	Israel (Haifa & Tel Aviv)	Royal Netherlands S.S. Co.	Amsterdam, Rotterdam or Antwerp every 3 weeks	£89 2s.
42-49 days	Cyprus, Lebanon & Egypt	Royal Netherlands S.S. Co.	Every fortnight	£89 2s.

UNION-CASTLE

TO

SOUTH, WEST & EAST AFRICA AND MAURITIUS

EAST AFRICAN SERVICE

s.s. "BRAEMAR CASTLE"

Sails from **LONDON** and is expected to take general cargo arriving alongside at the **KING GEORGE V DOCK (Shed 12)** from 13th FEBRUARY up to the evening of 19th FEBRUARY, for:—

		Arriving
GIBRALTAR	... ...	26 FEBRUARY
GENOA	... ...	28 FEBRUARY
ADEN	... ...	10 MARCH
MOMBASA	... ...	15 MARCH
ZANZIBAR	... ...	20 MARCH
DAR ES SALAAM	... ...	21 MARCH

also by transhipment for Mtwara and Seychelles.

Shippers are requested to note that all cargo is accepted by special arrangement only. Bookings must be made in advance, and no cargo should be despatched until receipt of a calling forward notice.

Shippers are reminded that on Saturday mornings cargo can be delivered only between the hours of 8 a.m. and 10 a.m.

GREENLY HOUSE,
30, Creechurch Lane, E.C.3

AVENUE 4343

31st January, 1963.

Braemar Castle sailing list, 1963.

| 29th Aug - 16th Sept | s.s. Orcades 18-day Mediterranean Cruise |

		Arrival		Departure		Hours in Port	Distance
Southampton				Saturday	29 August pm		1170
Ceuta	*for Tangier and Tetuan	Tuesday	1 September 8 am	Tuesday	1 September 7 pm	11	1653
Venice	*for the Lido, Cortina, Murano and Torcello	Saturday	5 September 8 am	Sunday	6 September noon	28	805
Naples	*for Rome, Pompeii, Amalfi, Sorrento, Baia, Vesuvius, Herculaneum, Capri and Ischia	Tuesday	8 September 7 am	Wednesday 9 September 1 am		18	581
Palma	*for Soller, Valldemosa, Porto Cristo, Manacor and Camp de Mar	Thursday	10 September 8 am	Thursday	10 September 7 pm	11	752
Lisbon	*for Sintra, Estoril, Pena Palace, Setubal, Mafra and Queluz	Saturday	12 September 8 am	Sunday	13 September noon	28	1024
London		Wednesday 16 September am					

*Excursions are available to these places. Dates and Ports of Call are subject to alteration without notice.

Orient Line *Orcades* cruise, 1959. *Orcades* was the first ship in the Orient Line rebuilding programme following the end of the Second World War. She was built in 1948 by Vickers Armstrong, and incorporated more features in her design than any other ship of her type. *Orcades* sailed on her maiden voyage from Southampton to Australia on 14 December 1948, with a passage time of twenty-eight days. In 1955 she was placed on the London–Panama–San Francisco–Vancouver–Auckland–Sydney–Suez–London route, and was transferred to the Pacific service in 1958. She was converted to a one-class vessel in 1964 and broken up in 1973.

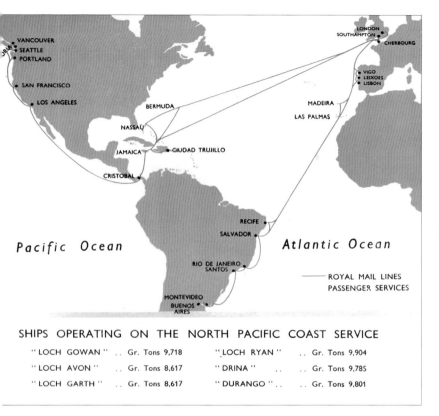

SHIPS OPERATING ON THE NORTH PACIFIC COAST SERVICE

"LOCH GOWAN"	.. Gr. Tons 9,718	"LOCH RYAN"	.. Gr. Tons 9,904
"LOCH AVON"	.. Gr. Tons 8,617	"DRINA" ..	.. Gr. Tons 9,785
"LOCH GARTH"	.. Gr. Tons 8,617	"DURANGO" ..	.. Gr. Tons 9,801

Royal Mail Lines cargo/passenger sailings, 1956.

Centaur in the Mersey, prior to her delivery voyage to Singapore on 20 January 1964. She was built for the service between Singapore and Australia, and operated on that route until 1982, when she left Fremantle on her final voyage on 15 September that year. She was then chartered to the St Helena Shipping Company for a year. *Centaur* was sold to Chinese interests in 1985, becoming *Hai Long* and *Hai Da* the following year. She survived until 1995, when she was scrapped at Xinhui, Guangdong, China.

Liverpool & North Wales Steamship Company's *St Trillo* off Llandudno Pier and in the Menai Straits. *St Trillo* originally operated on short cruises from Llandudno, in North Wales, to Anglesey for the Liverpool & North Wales Steamship Company. She was purchased by P&A Campbell for service in the Bristol Channel, converted to a floating restaurant in 1972, and broken up at Dublin three years later.

results of the National Seaman's Strike of 1966 had burdened the shipping operators with additional crew wages, there was a decline in demand, and other costs were rising in the early 1970s. *Queen Elizabeth 2*, *Carmania* and *Franconia* were the only passenger vessels owned by Cunard, and the returns of only 5 per cent were insufficient to fund replacement vessels.

It was during this period that containerisation was becoming popular, and Cunard became founder members of Associated Container Transport Limited through Port Line, with Blue Star Line, Ben Line, Ellerman and Harrison Line. The consortium of the five major shipping companies joined together to meet the high capital investment required in building and operating an innovative fleet of container ships. Cunard-Brocklebank was formed to manage and coordinate their cargo services. In 1971 Trafalgar House took over the Cunard Group, which had assets of £43 million.

Cunard Countess and *Cunard Conquest/Princess* were introduced in 1974. However, *Cunard Ambassador* suffered a major fire, and it was decided that it would be uneconomic to repair her, so she was sold, becoming a livestock carrier.

Mauretania was sold for scrapping in 1965; *Caronia*, *Carinthia* and *Sylvania* in 1968; *Iberia* in 1972; *Carmania*, *Franconia*, *Southern Cross* and *Chusan* in 1973; *Himalaya* and *Orsova* in 1974; *Northern Star*, *Ocean Monarch*, *Nevasa* and *Oronsay* in 1975; and *Arcadia* in 1979. Prior to *Canberra*'s maiden voyage on 2 June 1961, Sir Donald Anderson, Chairman of P&O, said,

> Any new passenger vessel must be designed to anticipate the future, if only because its 'life' is 20 to 30 years. But there are special difficulties in reading the crystal ball as regards *Canberra* and, for that matter, her Orient Line consort, the 42,000 ton *Oriana*. How can anyone be certain that these ships will be sound investments throughout a period of profound changes, political, social, commercial and technological? How can the passenger vessel hope to withstand the challenge of jet aircraft. Has ocean travel any future at all. The

answer is that ocean travel is not only a form of transport, it is also a holiday and a rest cure, a brief interlude of leisure, far from trials and tribulations.

Sir William Currie, former Chairman of P&O, added,

> In an age of supersonic air travel to come, passenger ships will be convalescent homes for the weary air traveller. Ship-owners are plainly convinced that there will always be many people who prefer to take their time and who intend to enjoy travelling; that such people will naturally prefer the ship to the aeroplane; and that they will be sufficient in number to keep the up-to-date passenger liner profitably employed.

However, questions were asked about why the firm should accept the commercial risk of a total investment of £30 million for the two passenger liners, as the volume of traffic showed a pronounced seasonal variation. The P&O board felt that the solution was the expanding economy, and resolved 'to widen their whole sphere of operations'.

P&O took delivery of the *Spirit of London* in 1972; she was built by Cantieri Navali del Tirreno e Reuniti at Genoa. She was originally ordered by Klosters Rederi A/S (Norwegian Caribbean Lines) and was purchased on the stocks. She had accommodation for 730 passengers, and was propelled by four diesel engines, which gave a service speed of 21 knots.

Canadian Pacific Steamships *Empress of Britain*, *Empress of England* and *Empress of Canada* were also employed cruising in the winter months and on the Canadian transatlantic service in the summer. The success of the Boeing 747 aircraft on long-haul routes had a significant effect on P&O-Orient Lines passenger services to Australia and New Zealand, with the line becoming P&O Cruises in 1973. Ships were sent there cruising, with *Oronsay* becoming very popular in the West Coast of America cruise market.

Chusan was used exclusively as a cruise ship from 1969, and *Himalaya* became popular in Australia after she undertook eight cruises between March and October 1968. *Himalaya* was replaced by *Arcadia* when she was sold for demolition in 1974. *Oriana* was designed to accommodate 638 first-class passengers and 1,496 in tourist class. *Canberra* could carry 556 First Class and 1,616 passengers in tourist class. Both liners were transferred to P&O Cruises in 1973, when they were designated as one-class vessels with a passenger capacity of 1,700 berths.

Canberra and *Oriana* then provided Mediterranean, Caribbean and world cruises, including fly-cruises from the United Kingdom. Princess Cruises was purchased by P&O in 1974; both companies continued to trade under their individual brand names, and Princess Cruises took over the Sitmar Line in 1988. The new *Oriana* was introduced in 1995, with *Aurora* following in 2000, and *Ocean Princess* and *Sea Princess* moving to P&O cruises and becoming *Oceana* and *Adonia*. P&O Princess Cruises merged with the Carnival Corporation in 2003, and the new *Arcadia* was introduced in 2005, with *Royal Princess* moving to P&O Cruises, becoming *Artemis*. *Adonia* moved back to Princess, and was renamed *Sea Princess*. *Ventura* entered service in 2008, *Artemis* was sold the following year and *Azura* joined the P&O Cruises fleet in 2010.

Shaw Savill Line withdrew the *Southern Cross* from her round-the-world schedule in 1971, and she was placed on a series of cruises from Liverpool before she was sold to Greek interests. Her sister *Northern Star* was also used for cruising but when it was found that she was uneconomic to operate she was sold and broken up. *Northern Star* suffered a number of mechanical problems, but *Southern Cross* went on to become a very successful cruise ship and survived until 2004, when she was finally broken up.

Royal Mail Lines' *Andes* carried out a number of cruises between 1956 and 1959, and was rebuilt for cruising as a one-class vessel with 480 berths by De Schelde at Flushing in 1959. She sailed on her first cruise in her new role on 10 June 1960. Her cargo facilities had been removed, a new 250-seat cinema was provided and air conditioning was installed. She was a very popular ship, but following boiler problems she was withdrawn and broken up at Ghent in 1971.

The Pacific Steam Navigation Company's *Reina del Mar* was built with first-class accommodation for 207 persons in single and two-berth rooms on 'C' and 'D' decks, including fourteen special two-berth rooms; all first-class rooms had their own private toilet and bath, hip bath or shower with hot and cold running water. On 'D' deck there were six deluxe cabins, each with a private shower and capable of conversion into a sitting room to form a suite when required. Each of these cabins was decorated in the theme of one of the countries served by the vessel.

Accommodation for the 216 cabin-class passengers was provided in single, two- and three-berth rooms. The walls in the first- and cabin-class accommodation were panelled in light-coloured wood veneers. The 343 tourist-class passengers were accommodated in single, two-, three-, four- and six-berth rooms on 'A' and 'B' decks. The first-class public rooms consisted of a restaurant seating 218 people, lounge, library, writing room, card room, cocktail bar and smoke room.

When the decline in passenger numbers was discussed by the PSNC Board in 1963, it was decided to charter the *Reina del Mar* to the Travel Savings Association, in which the company had a 25 per cent share. The other partners were British & Commonwealth Shipping Co. Ltd, Canadian Pacific Steamships Limited, and Mr Max Wilson. The chairman of the company told staff,

Apart from the sentimental angle, the sale of the ship is a forward step and one which should considerably strengthen the Company's financial position. We are relieved of the heavy losses which have been resulting from the ship's voyages and we will not have to provide depreciation for her; these two items

Summer services to the Isle of Man. The Isle of Man Steam Packet operated services and day cruises from Liverpool, Fleetwood and Heysham to the Isle of Man. When the Liverpool & North Wales Steamship Company went into liquidation in 1962, the Steam Packet also offered day cruises from Liverpool to Llandudno and Llandudno to Douglas, Isle of Man.

ISLE of MAN

1958 SUMMER SERVICES

THE ISLE OF MAN STEAM PACKET COMPANY LTD.
(Incorporated in the Isle of Man)

ATLANTIC HOLIDAYS

SEE U.S.A. & CANADA!

Here are holidays with a difference—Atlantic holidays by Cunard, which combine in one wonderful vacation two exciting travel adventures—a visit to the thrilling new world of the United States and Canada AND the pleasures of a voyage across the Atlantic in the luxurious comfort of a famous Cunarder.

Your local travel agent, or any Cunard ce, will give you a brochure detailing a variety interest-packed tours, all expertly designed how you in carefree comfort famous cities fascinating natural wonders in the United es and Canada.

TOUR ITINERARIES INCLUDE:

NEW YORK	BUFFALO
BOSTON	MONTREAL
WASHINGTON	PHILADELPHIA
PORTLAND	OTTAWA
WILLIAMSBURG	QUEBEC
PITTSBURGH	TORONTO
NIAGARA FALLS	

by *Cunard*

1959 Cunard Atlantic holiday advertisement.

ROYAL MAIL LINES

TO

SOUTH AMERICA

BRAZIL · URUGUAY
ARGENTINA

Also to

WEST INDIES
CENTRAL AMERICA
NORTH PACIFIC COAST

Cruises to
MEDITERRANEAN, NORWAY,
NORTHERN CAPITALS, WEST INDIES

R.M.S. "ANDES" is fitted with anti-roll stabilisers for maximum comfort at sea.

LONDON: Royal Mail House, Leadenhall Street, E.C.3
America House, Cockspur Street, S.W.I
SOUTHAMPTON: Royal Mail House, Terminus Terrace
LIVERPOOL: The P.S.N. Co. Pacific Building, James St. (2)

1958 Royal Mail Lines advertisement.

ELLERMAN GROUP

Linking **UNITED KINGDOM** and

NORTH EUROPEAN PORTS *with*
SOUTH and EAST AFRICA
SOUTH WEST AFRICA (Separate Direct Service)
ADEN and FAR EAST
ADEN and SABAH (Direct Service)
PORTUGAL, MEDITERRANEAN, LEVANT and BLACK SEA
★ EGYPT, RED SEA PORTS and PERSIAN GULF
★ INDIA, PAKISTAN, CEYLON and BURMA
★ AUSTRALIA

★ These destinations also NEW ZEALAND linked by regular services with Canada and U.S.A.

THE CITY LINE LTD.
75 Bothwell Street, Glasgow, C.2.
HALI LINE LTD.
Tower Building, Liverpool, 3.
ELLERMAN & BUCKNALL STEAMSHIP CO. LTD.
12/20 Camomile Street, London, E.C.3.
ELLERMAN & PAPAYANNI LINES LTD.
Tower Building, Liverpool, 3.
WESTCOTT & LAURANCE LINE LTD.
12/20 Camomile Street, London, E.C.3.

We serve the World

Ellerman Group advertisement.

Andes Sunshine Cruises, 1959.

LIVERPOOL

TO

ST. JOHN'S, Nfld., HALIFAX, N.S.
and BOSTON, U.S.A.

R.M.S. "NOVA SCOTIA"

Receiving Cargo ... ... 31st OCT. / 11th NOV.

R.M.S. "NEWFOUNDLAND"

Receiving Cargo ... ... 17th NOV. / 2nd DEC.

Loading Berth: SOUTH SIDE, HORNBY DOCK, LIVERPOOL.

THROUGH BILLS OF LADING issued to the interior of Newfoundland via St. John's Nfld., and to interior points of Canada and the U.S.A. via Halifax, N.S.

"SHIP VIA HALIFAX, N.S."

All bookings are subject to the conditions and exceptions of the Company's Bill of Lading.

The usual Customs papers Export Licences and Exchange Control Form (C.D.3), where required, MUST be in order before the goods are tendered for shipment.

REFRIGERATOR STOWAGE is available—subject to special engagement.

For Rates of Freight, Insurance and other information apply to:—

FURNESS, WITHY & CO. LTD.,
P.O. BOX 63
Royal Liver Building, Liverpool, 3.

Telephone: CENtral 9261

Telegrams:
Brantford, Liverpool, Telex
Telex No: 62441

or

FURNESS, WITHY & CO. LTD.,

GLASGOW C.1: 19 St. Vincent Place.
GRANGEMOUTH: 83 Lumley Street.
LEITH: Atlantic Chambers.

LONDON, E.C.3: 56 Leadenhall Street.
MIDDLESBROUGH: Lloyds Bank Chambers.
NEWCASTLE-ON-TYNE: Milburn House.

HOULDER BROS. & CO. LTD.,

BIRMINGHAM, 2: Waterloo House, Waterloo Street.
BRADFORD: 69 Market Street.
BRISTOL, 1: 49 Queens Square.
HANLEY: Halifax Chmbs., Market Sq.

HULL: Daily Mail Bldgs., Jameson St.
MANCHESTER, 2: 53 King Street.
SHEFFIELD, 1: Norfolk Chambers, Norfolk Row.

T. T. PASCOE LTD.,
CARDIFF: Crichton Hse., Mount Stuart Sq.

ALEX. M. HAMILTON & CO.,
BELFAST: 29/31 Waring Street.

R. M. BEVERIDGE & CO. LTD.,
DUNDEE: 54 Commercial Street.

Furness Warren Line's *Nova Scotia* and *Newfoundland*. Furness Warren Line operated passenger and cargo services from Liverpool to St John's–Newfoundland, Halifax–Nova Scotia and Boston by the *Newfoundland* and *Nova Scotia*. *Newfoundland* was built by Vickers Armstrong on the Tyne and came into service in 1948. She completed her last passenger voyage in 1961 on the route and was sold the following year, with her sister, to H. C. Sleigh Limited, and renamed *George Anson*. She arrived at Kaohsiung on 15 February 1971 to be broken up.

CONTINENTAL CRUISES

SCOTTISH LOCHS CRUISES

13-DAY CRUISE FROM HEYSHAM

DATE 1963		PORT	ARRIVE	DEPART
Wednesday	1 May	Heysham	—	16.00
Thursday	2 May	Cruising		
Friday	3 May	Stavanger	08.00	—
Saturday	4 May	Stavanger	—	08.00
		Cruise up Lyse Fjord		
Sunday	5 May	Copenhagen	14.00	—
Monday	6 May	Copenhagen		
Tuesday	7 May	Copenhagen	—	21.00
Wednesday	8 May	Kiel	09.00	—
Thursday	9 May	Kiel		
Friday	10 May	Kiel	—	05.00
		Through Kiel Canal		
Friday	10 May	Brunsbuttel	pass	16.30
Saturday	11 May	Ijmuiden	pass	08.30
Saturday	11 May	Amsterdam	11.00	—
Sunday	12 May	Amsterdam		
Monday	13 May	Amsterdam	—	22.00
Tuesday	14 May	Ijmuiden	pass	00.30
Tuesday	14 May	Harwich	09.00	

13-DAY CRUISE FROM HARWICH

DATE 1963		PORT	ARRIVE	DEPART
Thursday	16 May	Harwich	—	20.00
Friday	17 May	Ijmuiden	pass	07.30
Friday	17 May	Amsterdam	09.30	—
Saturday	18 May	Amsterdam		
Sunday	19 May	Amsterdam	—	16.00
Sunday	19 May	Ijmuiden	pass	18.30
Monday	20 May	Brunsbuttel	pass	09.30
		Through Kiel Canal		
Monday	20 May	Kiel	17.00	—
Tuesday	21 May	Kiel		
Wednesday	22 May	Kiel	—	04.00
Wednesday	22 May	Copenhagen	13.00	—
Thursday	23 May	Copenhagen		
Friday	24 May	Copenhagen	—	10.00
Saturday	25 May	Stavanger	16.00	—
		Cruise up Lyse Fjord		
Sunday	26 May	Stavanger		
Monday	27 May	Stavanger	—	05.00
Tuesday	28 May	Cruising		
Wednesday	29 May	Heysham	09.00	

6-DAY SUMMER CRUISE FROM HEYSHAM

DATE 1963		PORT	ARRIVE	DEPART
Wednesday	5 June	Heysham	—	17.00
Thursday	6 June	Ashnish	08.00	15.00
Thursday	6 June	Craignure		
Friday	7 June	Tobermory	08.00	14.00
Friday	7 June	Loch Bay		
Saturday	8 June	Portree	11.00	19.00
Saturday	8 June	Loch Alsh		*
Sunday	9 June	Cruising		
Sunday	9 June	Brodick	18.00	—
Monday	10 June	Brodick		21.00
Tuesday	11 June	Heysham	08.00	

* Overnight anchorage, passengers stay aboard.

10-DAY SUMMER CRUISE FROM HEYSHAM

DATE 1963		PORT	ARRIVE	DEPART
Friday	14 June	Heysham	—	17.00
Saturday	15 June	Iona	08.00	13.30
Saturday	15 June	Tobermory	15.30	—
Sunday	16 June	Tobermory	—	08.00
Sunday	16 June	Cruising		
Sunday	16 June	Ardmore (Skye)		
Monday	17 June	Tarbert (Harris)	08.30	13.30
Monday	17 June	Stornoway	16.00	—
Tuesday	18 June	Stornoway	—	18.00
Tuesday	18 June	Broad Bay		
Wednesday	19 June	Ullapool	noon	—
Thursday	20 June	Ullapool	—	08.00
Thursday	20 June	Gairloch	11.00	—
Friday	21 June	Gairloch	—	08.00
Friday	21 June	Portree	11.00	19.00
Friday	21 June	Loch Alsh		*
Saturday	22 June	Cruising		
Saturday	22 June	Proag Bay		
Sunday	23 June	Brodick	noon	21.30
Monday	24 June	Heysham	08.30	

Above:
Amsterdam

Below left:
Stavanger Cathedral

Below right:
Copenhagen,
City Hall Square

Duke of Lancaster cruises, 1963. *Duke of Lancaster*, *Duke of Rothesay* and *Duke of Argyll* were built for the service between Heysham and Belfast. *Duke of Lancaster* was designed to be able to provide short cruises from Heysham and Harwich, mainly to the Scottish lochs and islands, and also some Continental cruises. Prices ranged from £95 per person for a Cabin de luxe, to £50 for a place in a double-berth cabin. She was built in 1956, and spent most her career in this dual role until 1969, when she was converted to a stern-loading car ferry. When the Heysham–Belfast service was closed on 6 April 1975, she was transferred to the Fishguard–Rosslare and Holyhead–Dun Laoghaire routes, and was laid up at Holyhead at the end of 1978. The following year she was moved and laid up at Barrow, and in August that year she was towed to Mostyn, North Wales, and beached at Llanerch-y-Mor. Her purchaser, Empirewise Limited of Liverpool, intended to convert her into a leisure centre and hotel but problems arose over obtaining planning permission for the venture. She was renamed *Duke of Llanerch-y-Mor*, and opened briefly in a leisure role, but the plans have never been developed and she is still moored in that position, near the River Dee.

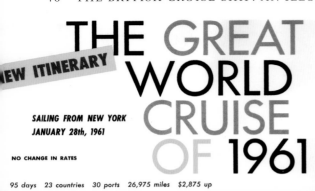

THE GREAT WORLD CRUISE OF 1961

NEW ITINERARY

**SAILING FROM NEW YORK
JANUARY 28th, 1961**

NO CHANGE IN RATES

95 days   23 countries   30 ports   26,975 miles $2,875 up

Cunard's famous cruise liner CARONIA

CUNARD LINE

The Great World Cruise of 1961 by the Cunard liner *Caronia*.

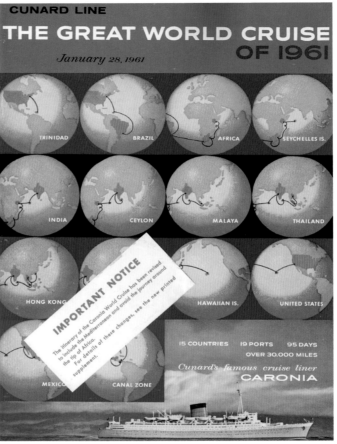

CUNARD LINE

THE GREAT WORLD CRUISE OF 1961

January 28, 1961

TRINIDAD   BRAZIL   AFRICA   SEYCHELLES IS.

INDIA   CEYLON   MALAYA   THAILAND

HONG KONG   JAPAN   HAWAIIAN IS.   UNITED STATES

MEXICO   CANAL ZONE

IMPORTANT NOTICE

The itinerary of the Caronia World Cruise has been revised to include the Mediterranean and avoid the journey around the tip of Africa. For details of these changes, see the new printed supplement.

15 COUNTRIES   19 PORTS   95 DAYS
OVER 30,000 MILES

Cunard's famous cruise liner CARONIA

CRUISE PROGRAM

COUNTRY	PORT	MILEAGE	ARRIVE	DEP
	NEW YORK (Embark 8:00 p.m. to 11:00 p.m.)			Jan. 28
CANARY ISLANDS	LAS PALMAS	2959	Feb. 4th AM	Feb. 5
MADEIRA	FUNCHAL	282	Feb. 6th AM	Feb. 6
MOROCCO	TANGIER	638	Feb. 8th AM	Feb. 8
SPAIN	MALAGA	90	Feb. 9th AM	Feb. 1
BALEARIC ISLANDS	PALMA	400	Feb. 11th AM	Feb. 1
SPAIN	BARCELONA	133	Feb. 12th AM	Feb. 1
FRANCE	VILLEFRANCHE	270	Feb. 13th AM	Feb. 14
ITALY	NAPLES	368	Feb. 15th PM	Feb. 1
SICILY	MESSINA	175	Feb. 19th AM	Feb. 1
	CATANIA	48	Feb. 19th PM	Feb. 1
MALTA	VALLETTA	110	Feb. 20th AM	Feb. 2
GREECE	ATHENS	517	Feb. 22nd AM	Feb. 2
DODECANESE ISLANDS	RHODES	257	Feb. 24th AM	Feb. 2
EGYPT	ALEXANDRIA	330	Feb. 25th AM	Feb. 2
	PORT SAID	156	Feb. 28th AM	Feb. 2
			Transiting the Suez Canal	
	SUEZ	87	Feb. 28th PM	Mar.
THE SUDAN	PORT SUDAN	694	Mar. 3rd AM	Mar.
ADEN	ADEN	658	Mar. 5th AM	Mar.
INDIA	BOMBAY	1657	Mar. 9th AM	Mar. 1
CEYLON	COLOMBO	889	Mar. 17th AM	Mar. 1
MALAYA	SINGAPORE	1567	Mar. 22nd AM	Mar. 2
THAILAND	BANGKOK	800	Mar. 25th AM	Mar. 2
HONG KONG	HONG KONG	1458	Mar. 29th AM	Mar. 3
JAPAN	KOBE	1515	Apr. 3rd AM	Apr.
	YOKOHAMA	350	Apr. 6th AM	Apr.
HAWAIIAN ISLANDS	HONOLULU	3409	Apr. 15th AM	Apr. 1
UNITED STATES	LONG BEACH	2228	Apr. 21st AM	Apr. 2
MEXICO	ACAPULCO	1502	Apr. 25th AM	Apr. 2
CANAL ZONE	BALBOA	1428	Apr. 28th PM	Apr. 2
			Transiting the Panama Canal	
	CRISTOBAL	44	Apr. 29th PM	Apr. 2
UNITED STATES	NEW YORK	1956	May 3rd PM	

Thos. Cook & Son are offering Shore Arrangements at most of the new po
call. Details of these will be available through your travel agent. From Be
on all Shore Arrangements will remain the same—consult the Shore Pr
booklet for details.

Empress of Canada in the Mersey.

Direct Cruises' *Apollon* enters Langton Dock at Liverpool.

CPR sailing list for
maiden voyage of
Empress of Canada.

Canadian Pacific

MAIDEN VOYAGE

EMPRESS OF CANADA

LIVERPOOL - QUEBEC & MONTREAL · MONDAY, APRIL 24, 1961

Receiving Cargo April 15 - April 20.
Loading Berth—North No. 1 Gladstone Dock, Liverpool.

SUPERB PASSENGER ACCOMMODATION—FULLY AIR-CONDITIONED—
FIRST CLASS AND TOURIST. SHIPPERS' ENQUIRIES DIRECT OR THROUGH
THEIR USUAL AGENTS, WILL RECEIVE IMMEDIATE ATTENTION

FAST SERVICE: This vessel is scheduled to maintain a six days' passage between Liverpool and Montreal.

THROUGH BILLS OF LADING: Through Bills of Lading are issued to inland destinations in Canada and U.S.A.

CANADIAN PACIFIC EXPRESS: Merchandise, samples, livestock and valuables sent by Express Service to all parts of Canada and U.S.A.

Goods are received for shipment only subject to the terms and conditions of the Company's usual form of Wharfinger's receipt and/or Bill of Lading.

For rates and information apply:—

CANADIAN PACIFIC RAILWAY CO.

Royal Liver Building, Liverpool, or any other
Canadian Pacific Office, a list of which is overleaf.

Subject to change without notice

Media was the first new vessel built for the Cunard Line following the Second World War. She sailed on her maiden voyage from Liverpool to New York on 20 August 1947. She was fitted with stabilisers in 1952 when her promenade deck was glazed. *Media* and her sister ship *Parthia* were dual cargo-passenger vessels, and it became uneconomical to operate them. Her last passenger sailing for the Cunard Line was in September 1961 from Liverpool to Quebec and Montreal. She was sold to Cogeder Line, Genoa, in 1961 and was modernised and rebuilt by Officine A&R Navi at Genoa, renamed *Flavia*, and was able to accommodate 1,224 passengers in one class. *Flavia* was initially employed on the Genoa–Australia, and later Bremerhaven–Southampton–Australia, route. In 1968 she was cruising in the Mediterranean, with winter cruises in the Caribbean. The following year she was sold to Costa Armatori S.p.A of Naples and cruised out of Miami. She was sold to Flavian Shipping S.A. Panama, renamed *Flavian* and laid up at Hong Kong in 1982. In 1986 she was purchased by Lavia Shipping of Panama, renamed *Lavia* and again laid up at Hong Kong. On 7 January 1989 she suffered a serious fire, and was beached and declared a total loss.

The New Zealand Shipping Company passenger liner *Remuera* sails on her first voyage for the company from Princes Landing Stage, Liverpool, in 1962. She was built for the Cunard Line as *Parthia* and was transferred to the Eastern & Australian Steamship Company in 1965, becoming *Aramac*, for the Melbourne–Hong Kong and Japan service. She was broken up at Kaohsiung in 1969.

LISBON	ii	*Renowned seafarers' capital city on seven hills*		AUCKLAND	x	*Sub-tropical parkland on mountainous isthmus*
GIBRALTAR	ii	*British citadel named after Arab corsair*		SUVA	xi	*Well-planned capital of Fiji Islands*
NAPLES	iii	*Unforgettable setting for drama of past and present*		HONOLULU	xi	*Featuring only royal palace in United States*
MALTA, GC	iii	*The valiant island*		VANCOUVER	xii	*Angler's Valhalla in shadow of ski-er's Utopia*
PORT SAID	iv	*Memories of international banquet for 6,000*		SAN FRANCISCO	xiii	*Sunshine city by the Golden Gate*
ADEN	iv	*Oil-fuelling port on volcanic peninsula*		LOS ANGELES	xiii	*Exotic paradise with unsurpassed climate*
COLOMBO	iv	*Great seaport and unique Oriental market*		YOKOHAMA	xiv	*Traditional enchantment amid Western moderni*
FREMANTLE	v	*Desert State's window on the world*		KOBE	xiv	*Trading centre established 18 centuries ago*
ADELAIDE	v	*Carnivals, vineyards, and shape of towns to come*		HONGKONG	xiv	*'Walled village of the flowered lagoon'*
MELBOURNE	vi	*Elegant design for gracious living*		MANILA	xv	*Polyglot focus of contrasts*
SYDNEY	vii	*Vigorous metropolis on incomparable harbour*		SINGAPORE	xv	*Glittering emporium at Orient's cross-roads*

Canberra maiden voyage.

above—Princess Room   *above—First class restaurant*
below—First class two-berth cabin   *below—In the Penthouse Suite*

Canberra and *Oriana* 1961.

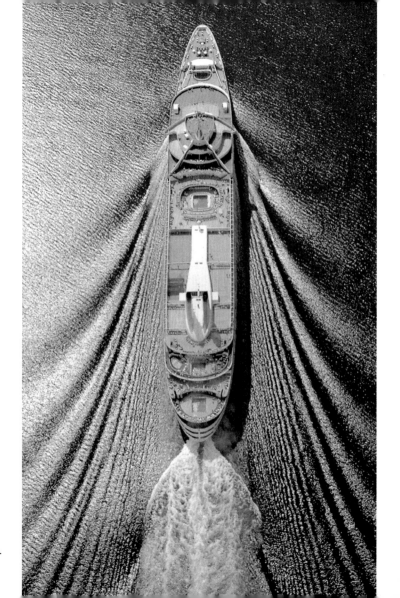

Canberra.

alone amount to a very considerable sum. I therefore view the future with equanimity and indeed with enthusiasm, and have no hesitation in stating that there is no need for despondency.

The Union Castle Line took over the management of the liner for the period of this project, and offered cruises from the United Kingdom, as well as providing voyages in the South African market to South American ports. Union Castle used *Stirling Castle* and *Capetown Castle* on cruises at the end of their careers.

Travel Savings Association chartered the *Empress of Britain*, *Empress of England*, *Stratheden* and the *Reina del Mar*. *Stratheden* completed only four cruises, but those operated by *Reina del Mar* and *Empress of England* included the New York Trade Fair and the 1964 Tokyo Olympics. The *Empress of Britain* was withdrawn in 1964, and the Travel Savings Association collapsed the following year. *Empress of England* was sold to the Shaw Savill Line in 1970 and renamed *Ocean Monarch*; she received a £2-million upgrade and conversion by Cammell Laird at Birkenhead. However, she also suffered mechanical problems, and was withdrawn and sold to be broken up in 1974.

Max Wilson had written about his pioneering ideas of sea travel in 1962, claiming that 'everyone in this country, and others with long standing ties with Britain, is a potential sea traveller. If the shipping lines are not getting these travellers it is largely their own fault.' He claimed that the fundamental weakness at the time was the care of the passenger, particularly in the provision of good standards of food, services and variety of entertainment. He felt that many shipping people regarded a sea voyage as little more than the transport of passengers, and that this was the wrong attitude, as a voyage on a ship should be seen as

a holiday in itself or the beginning of a holiday, even if the primary purpose of a passenger is to travel from one destination to another then the ship-owner must devote his energy and imagination into making it a holiday. There are still those diehards in the industry who regard passengers as a necessary evil.

Wilson felt that entertainment was one of the most important issues on cruise ships, and he conducted interviews with 200 people who told him that they found much of the voyage dull and boring, and at times they did not know what to do with themselves. During his initial charters of passenger ships he had a special cabaret and band flown out from Britain to entertain the passengers. He employed calypso singers during cocktail hour, and even arranged to fly out a different cabaret at the last port of call before Southampton so that passengers had a change in entertainment for the last three days of the voyage. He also organised large prizes to encourage passengers to take part in fancy dress competitions and other activities. He recognised that

another vital part of a sea voyage is food. I doubt if it is necessary to give elaborate meals and menus. What the average passenger wants is good food, well cooked and attractively presented. There is room for much thought. Why not a charcoal grill on deck, with steak and salad only. Against tropical skies, and with skilful lighting effects and atmosphere, it could be most attractive and could easily be done.

Wilson thought that the standard of service provided was equally important as 'the airlines go to a great deal of trouble to choose the right stewards and stewardesses, and train them to look after passengers really well'. He thought that the standard of civility, from pursers to cabin boys, left a lot to be desired, and that complaints should be taken more seriously and used in a positive way to train future staff. The shipping lines 'should be prepared to introduce stewards and stewardesses from any part of the world who will give their passengers a better service. If the British seaman does not wish to compete, then he must find other work.'

He also looked at the management and planning aspects of cruising and felt that

> shipping lines could do very much more in the field of sales and promotion. Ports of call should be as interesting as possible and should be varied from one voyage to another. No shipping company, so far as I am concerned has really gone out of its way to create new traffic. It is high time they did to regain some of the traffic they have lost to the airlines. However, the price should be right and there is no reason why a fortnight's holiday on a ship should cost more than a good holiday ashore.

The lack of imagination and enterprise was the main reason for the failure to create new traffic, according to Wilson, 'not only in the shipping companies, but in the travel agencies that serve them'. He felt the key was to find out what the public want and 'when a shipping company can get its passengers to their destination feeling that they have had a wonderful time, that it has been just what they wanted, and that they don't want to get off, and then passenger ship problems will be largely solved'.

Princess Cruises were taken over by P&O in 1974 from Stanley B. McDonald, who had founded the line by chartering the Canadian Pacific Alaska cruise ship *Princess Patricia* for Mexican Riviera cruises from Los Angeles. However, when the *Princess Patricia* proved unsuitable, the company used *Italia* for the service. She had been designed by Gustavo Finali and Romano Boico, who had created interiors for the Italian Line's *Augustus* and *Raffaello* and Home Line's *Oceanic* and *Homeric*. The charter was ended in 1973 and the Costa's *Carla C* replaced her. P&O purchased *Sea Venture* and *Island Venture*, renaming them *Pacific Princess* and *Island Princess*; both vessels were the subject of a television series, *The Love Boat*, in 1977. *Spirit of London* was transferred and renamed *Sun Princess*. The acquisition of

Princess Cruises enabled P&O to regain a foothold in the American cruise market, and the television series helped to create a new image for the cruise industry as 'fun ships', which was extended and reinforced by Ted Arison when he formed Carnival Cruise Lines. Prior to that there had been a rather formal approach to cruising, which had limited its appeal, and the publicity from the television series gave people the opportunity to see another side to the industry.

UK Owned & Registered Fleet (Trading Ships 500 grt & over) 31st March 1982
(30th June 1981 figures in brackets)

Ship Type	No.	dwt (000)
Passenger/Cargo	92 (99)	169 (177)
Cellular Container	68 (72)	1462 (1500)
Other Cargo Liner	156 (191)	1863 (2196)
Total Liner	316 (362)	3494 (3873)
Bulk Carrier	290 (309)	7495 (7818)
Other Tramp	45 (49)	220 (258)
Total Tramp	335 (358)	7715 (8076)
Tanker	327 (362)	18385 (21293)
Total All Ships	978 (1082)	29593 (33241)

Dept. of Industry

Booth Line advert.

BOOTH LINE

REGULAR CARGO & MAIL SERVICES

LIVERPOOL and PORTUGAL to BARBADOS and TRINIDAD
(also for Leeward and Windward Isles with transhipment)

●

NEW YORK to Bermuda, West Indies, North and mid-Brazil, Bolivia, Leticia and Iquitos

●

LIVERPOOL to LEIXÕES, LISBON and MADEIRA

ROUND VOYAGES
1,000 Miles up the River AMAZON
Call at Leixões (Oporto), Lisbon, Madeira, Barbados, and Trinidad.
USING THE SHIP AS HOTEL

LIVERPOOL, LONDON and ANTWERP to
Belem, Manaus, Sao Luis, Parnaiba, Fortaleza, Bolivia and Iquitos

THE BOOTH STEAMSHIP CO. Ltd
Cunard Building, LIVERPOOL 3. Tel. Cen. 9181

London Passenger Office: 3 Lower Regent St., LONDON, S.W.1. Tel. WHI 2266
London Agents (Cargo): LAMPORT & HOLT LINE LTD.,
31/33 Lime Street, E.C.3. Tel. Mansion House 7533

Booth Line, 1961. Booth Line ships provided a regular first- and tourist-class passenger service between the United Kingdom and the West Indies islands of Barbados and Trinidad. There were calls at Leixoes, Lisbon and Madeira, both northwards and southwards. Round voyages were also offered 1,000 miles up the River Amazon, with passengers able to use the ship as a hotel at Manaus.

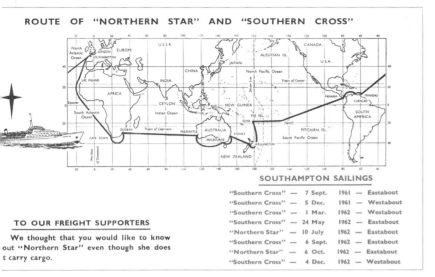

ROUTE OF "NORTHERN STAR" AND "SOUTHERN CROSS"

SOUTHAMPTON SAILINGS

"Southern Cross" —	7 Sept.	1961 —	Eastabout
"Southern Cross" —	5 Dec.	1961 —	Westabout
"Southern Cross" —	1 Mar.	1962 —	Westabout
"Southern Cross" —	24 May	1962 —	Eastabout
"Northern Star" —	10 July	1962 —	Eastabout
"Southern Cross" —	6 Sept.	1962 —	Eastabout
"Northern Star" —	6 Oct.	1962 —	Eastabout
"Southern Cross" —	4 Dec.	1962 —	Westabout

TO OUR FREIGHT SUPPORTERS

We thought that you would like to know out "Northern Star" even though she does t carry cargo.

Northern Star and *Southern Cross* sailing details, 1961/1962.

Hubert was built by Cammell Laird for the Booth Line in 1955. She sailed on her maiden voyage on 11 February from Liverpool to Leixoes, Lisbon, Madeira, Barbados, Para and Manaus. She provided accommodation for seventy-four first- and ninety-six tourist-class passengers, and was popular with passengers cruising up the Amazon to Manaus. In 1964 she was transferred to the Blue Star Line and chartered to Austasia Limited as the *Malaysia*. She was sold in 1976, converted to a cattle carrier and given the name *Khalij Express*. She was broken up at Port Alang in 1984.

Northern Star sailed on her maiden voyage from Southampton on 10 July 1962, with over 1,400 passengers and 480 crew on board. She was employed with her sister, *Southern Cross*, on round-the-world voyages until she was withdrawn from service in 1975 and sold to the ship-breakers. She arrived at Taiwan on 11 December that year to be broken up.

Landing at Iona

IONA A place of pilgrimage, birthplace of Scottish Christianity, burial ground of Kings. It is beautiful and it is unique. Its atmosphere cannot be equalled anywhere in the world. Not to be missed.

RMS "KING GEORGE V"

VITAL STATISTICS

Built: 1926, Wm. Denny & Bros. Ltd., Dumbarton
Length: 270 feet
Tonnage: 985
Type: Turbine — 2 screws

CATERING

Excellent meals are served in "King George V's" spacious dining saloon.
Teas, coffees, scones and cakes are available in the cafeteria at popular prices.
The ship is fully licensed.

TP639 40M 4/73

Majestic Cruising by "King George V"

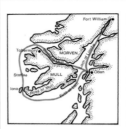

Caledonian MacBrayne

Sacred Isle Cruise

STAFFA and IONA on Mondays, Tuesdays, Thursdays and Saturdays.
IONA on Wednesdays.

On Mondays, Tuesdays, Thursdays and Saturdays the steamer sails from O through the Sound of Mull to Tobermory then by the west coast of Mull to St where she will pass close to the caves to give the best possible view, and then to the Sacred Isle of Iona, where passengers are landed by ferry boat. The re journey is made via the south of Mull.

On Wednesdays the steamer sails from Fort William down Loch Linnhe to Oban then via the Firth of Lorne and Ross of Mull to Iona before returning by the same ro

	Oban	Tobermory	Iona		Iona	Oban	
Mondays, Tuesdays, Thursdays and Saturdays, 21 May until 15 September	1000 →	1145 →	1400		1630 →	1900	

	Fort William	Oban	Iona		Iona	Oban	Fort William
Wednesdays, 23 May until 12 September	0845 →	1045 →	1330		1515 →	1745 →	2000

Six Lochs Cruise

Commencing at Oban the steamer sails southward through the Sound of Kerrera the Islands of Seil and Luing to Loch Melfort, then on to Lochs Craignish and Cr before turning westward to Loch Buie through the Gulf of Corryvreckan, site of famous whirlpool.

From Loch Buie she sails northward by Lismore to Lochs Linnhe and Corry be returning to Oban.

Sundays, 1 July until 26 August.

Leave Oban 1100, arrive back 1800. On occasions, route may be reversed.

OBAN – FORT WILLIAM

Wednesdays and Fridays, 23 May until 14 September

Outward	F	A	B	Inward	W	F	A	B	W
Oban	1000	1700	1800	Fort William	0845	1400	1905	2005	2005
‡Appin†	1030	1730	1830	‡Appin†	—	1520	—	—	—
Fort William	1200	1900	2000	Oban	1045	1600	2105	2205	2205

Code: ‡ By arrangement † Passengers are transferred from and to the steamer by ferry boat A—Fridays only from 7 September B—Fridays only until 31 August W—Wednesday only F—Friday only

EVENING CRUISE TO FORT WILLIAM
(no landing)

Wednesdays, 23 May until 12 Septem
leave Oban 1800, arrive back 2205

Fridays, 25 May until 31 August,
leave Oban 1800, arrive back 2205

Fridays, 7 and 14 September only,
leave Oban 1700, arrive back 2205

Caledonian MacBrayne *King George V* cruises.

Cruise details.

A new idea in cruising holidays

TSA brochure, 1963/64.

YOU ENJOY
THE BEST OF EVERYTHING

Queen Mary.

Pacific Steam Navigation Company *Reina del Mar* brochure, 1963.

1966 *Queen Mary* Washington Birthday Cruise.

Above and below: Empress of Canada *Caribbean cruise, 6 March 1965.*

Aureol in the Mersey. Elder Dempster Lines' *Aureol* was built in 1951 for their service from Liverpool to West Africa. Her sister ships on the service were sold by 1968, and *Aureol* made the last West African passenger sailing from Liverpool on 16 March 1972, before being transferred to Southampton. However, she was laid up in 1974 and sold the following year, becoming *Marianna VI* for use as an accommodation ship at Jeddah. She was overhauled at Piraeus in 1979, and berthed at Rabegh in 1980 to operate as an accommodation ship. In 1991 she was laid up off Piraeus and was broken up at Alang ten years later.

Carmania and *Chusan* at Valetta, Malta.

Anchor Line *Circassia* lounge. *Circassia* was built in 1937 and sailed on her maiden voyage to Bombay. In 1940 she was converted to an Armed Merchant Cruiser, became a troopship in 1942, and a Landing Ship Infantry in 1943. She resumed Anchor Line service in 1947 and made the line's final passenger sailing from Glasgow and Birkenhead to Bombay on 13 January 1966. She was broken up at Alicante on her return.

Left: Sylvania was built for the Cunard Line by John Brown & Company on the Clyde in 1957. She replaced *Britannic* on the Liverpool–New York route, and in 1965, made the first Cunard cruise out of Liverpool since 1939. During her overhaul in 1967 she had her hull painted white, and was sold to the Sitmar Line in 1968, becoming *Fairwind*. In 1988 she was sold and renamed *Dawn Princess* for Princess Cruises, becoming *Albatros* in 1994. She returned to the Mersey on one occasion while named *Albatros*. She was broken up at Alang in 2004.

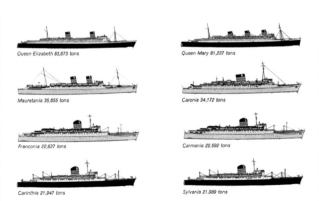

Cunard Line.

Right: Caronia World Cruise, 1967.

Cunard Line

the **1967** great

WORLD CRUISE

Aboard the

CARONIA

Sailing from

NEW YORK January 26, 1967

FORT LAUDERDALE January 30, 1967

AIR-CONDITIONED

Queen Mary.

Queen Elizabeth 2 at Los Angeles.

Right: Midland Bank cruise advert, 1967.

We've served Cunard passengers on almost 2,000 round trips

The Midland Bank first opened branches in Cunard liners in the Twenties . . . starting with the Berengaria. Since then, we've served Cunard passengers on over 12 million miles of round trips across the Atlantic. Nearly two thousand journeys. You will find the same thoughtful, expert service aboard the Q4, and get the benefit of nearly 50 years of sea-going banking experience, whether you are a Midland Bank customer or not.

Midland Bank

HEAD OFFICE: POULTRY, LONDON, E.C.2.

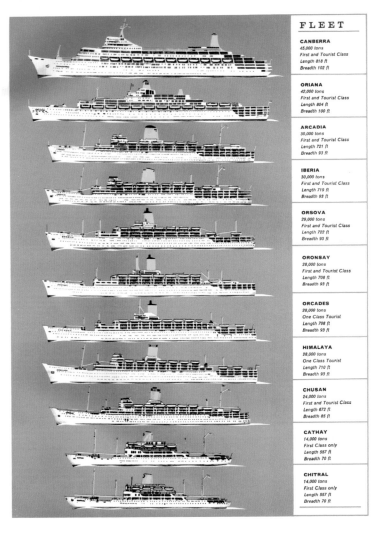

Carmania. *Carmania* was built as *Saxonia* at the yard of John Brown & Co. Ltd on the Clyde. She was launched by Lady Churchill on 17 February 1954 and sailed on her maiden voyage from Liverpool to Montreal on 2 September that year. She was the first of four sisters built for the Cunard Line service to Quebec and Montreal. In 1961 she was employed on the London–New York service and cruised out of Port Everglades in the winter months. She returned to her builders in 1962 to be converted to a dual-purpose North Atlantic cruise liner, painted *Caronia* green and renamed *Carmania*. Between 1964 and 1970 she was employed on 'fly-cruises' in the Mediterranean in the summer, and Caribbean cruises in the winter months, and was painted white in 1967. *Carmania* was laid up at Southampton in 1971 and was moored in the River Fal in 1972. She was sold to Nikreis Maritime Corporation in 1973 and renamed *Leonid Sobinov*, managed by CTC Lines for the Southampton–Australia and New Zealand service and for cruising duties. On 24 November 1975 she was the first passenger liner to pass through the newly reopened Suez Canal after its clearance following the 1967 war. After the invasion of Afghanistan by Russian troops, she was precluded from operating from Australia in 1979, and sailed on services for the Russian Far East Shipping Company. As *Leonid Sobinov* she operated a variety of services and cruises until 1999, when she was delivered to Indian ship-breakers at Alang on 1 October that year. She had been anchored off Alang since 1 April.

P&O Fleet in 1967.

FLEET

CANBERRA
45,000 tons
First and Tourist Class
Length 818 ft
Breadth 102 ft

ORIANA
42,000 tons
First and Tourist Class
Length 804 ft
Breadth 100 ft

ARCADIA
30,000 tons
First and Tourist Class
Length 721 ft
Breadth 93 ft

IBERIA
30,000 tons
First and Tourist Class
Length 719 ft
Breadth 93 ft

ORSOVA
29,000 tons
First and Tourist Class
Length 722 ft
Breadth 93 ft

ORONSAY
28,000 tons
First and Tourist Class
Length 708 ft
Breadth 93 ft

ORCADES
28,000 tons
One Class Tourist
Length 708 ft
Breadth 93 ft

HIMALAYA
28,000 tons
One Class Tourist
Length 710 ft
Breadth 93 ft

CHUSAN
24,000 tons
First and Tourist Class
Length 672 ft
Breadth 85 ft

CATHAY
14,000 tons
First Class only
Length 557 ft
Breadth 70 ft

CHITRAL
14,000 tons
First Class only
Length 557 ft
Breadth 70 ft

Carmania pool and sun deck.

P. & A. Campbell's *Bristol Queen*.

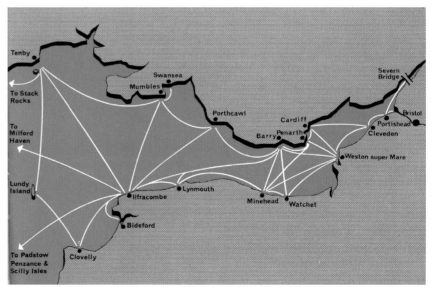

P. & A. Campbell's Bristol Channel routes. Cruising in the Bristol Channel was a popular pastime, with thousands who enjoyed the many two- or three-hour morning or afternoon cruises, such as those from Ilfracombe to Bideford Bay, or from Weston or Barry along the coast to the Channel lightships; or around Steep or Flat Holm; or from other ports in the Channel to nearby destinations; or whole day trips from Bristol or South Wales ports to Ilfracombe; or the shorter excursions from Cardiff, Weston or Clevedon to see the Severn Bridge.

	December 1975 No.	December 1975 mn.dwt.	December 1980 No.	December 1980 mn.dwt.	June 1985 No.	June 1985 mn.dwt.
TANKERS	454	30.0	381	23.3	214	9.8
DRY BULK CARRIERS	546	14.3	374	8.1	215	4.3
PASSENGER FERRIES/ CRUISE SHIPS	112	0.2	100	0.2	83	0.2
CELLULAR CONTAINER SHIPS	89	1.3	71	1.5	52	1.4
CARGO LINERS	413	4.1	215	2.5	83	1.0
TOTAL	1,614	50.0	1,141	35.6	647	16.6

The General Council of Shipping reported in 1982 that

the passenger cruise ships of today are the successors to the passenger liners of the past. Though British deep sea cruise ships are now concentrated in the hands of only two owners, they are both efficient and successful operators, and their 10 ships offer a range of cruises in all parts of the world. For those in a hurry to reach the sun, there are cruises which the passenger can fly out to join in the Mediterranean. One of the ships which offers this sort of cruise for part of the year is P&O's *Uganda*. The Cunard ships, led by the *Queen Elizabeth 2*, vary their programmes, but they are usually to be found in the Caribbean or off North America, normally on the Atlantic, but sometimes using Los Angeles as a base on the North American western seaboard. The three P&O 'Princess' ships cruising out of US ports cover sharply contrasting regions – Mexico, Alaska and the Caribbean, or even the Polynesian world of the South Pacific. Australia is also a base for *Oriana* and, for part of the year by *Canberra*. These ships earn major sums of foreign currency for the United Kingdom, and their popularity has encouraged investment in new ships. *Canberra*, *Queen*

Elizabeth 2 and *Uganda* returned to the UK from the Task Force in the South Atlantic to their regular task of serving the thousands who believe that there is no better holiday in the world than cruising on a British passenger ship.

Royal Mail Lines were appointed the United Kingdom general passenger agent for all passenger services operated by the various Russian shipping lines. Through the Furness Withy Group's main passenger offices in Haymarket, London, control was exercised over all reservations for Russian main-line services to Leningrad and to Montreal, as well as for the many cruises operated by Russian passenger ships. The group extended its hotel-owning interests, and through Shaw Savill it controlled Saxon Inns, a company that ran motels at Harlow, Whitley Bridge in Yorkshire, Huddersfield, Blackburn and Northampton. Shaw Savill also had interests in a number of hotels in New Zealand. Another member of the group, Houlder Brothers, owned a hotel at Malindi on the Indian Ocean coast of Kenya, and another in the Seychelles. Houlder World Holidays specialised in long-distance holidays by air, organising trips to East Africa, the Pacific Islands, Sri Lanka, the Far East and North America.

Trafalgar House made an unsuccessful takeover bid for P&O in 1983 after they had acquired 4.9 per cent of the shares, and Cunard took over Norwegian Cruise Lines vessels *Sagafjord* and *Vistafjord*. Both vessels retained their names and Norwegian crew, but were painted with Cunard funnel colours. They were built for the Oslo–New York transatlantic service. *Sagafjord* and *Vistafjord* were employed initially on Pacific cruising, and both deputised for *Queen Elizabeth 2* in 1986, when she was converted to diesel propulsion.

Sea Goddess I and *Sea Goddess II* were also taken over in 1986 on a twelve-year charter with an option to purchase. They had been owned by Norske Cruises and marketed as Sea Goddess Cruises in the luxury cruise market. Passenger booking figures dropped following the bombing at Libya; the shipyard were owed $50 million and threatened to repossess the vessels. Following negotiations, the Midland Bank took over the debt, and the ships were chartered to Cunard.

Hebridean Island Cruises was established in 1989 with a converted Scottish Western Isles ferry to offer five-star luxury cruising at the highest level of service. Cruises by the *Hebridean Princess* are mainly around the Scottish Islands and Northern Ireland, but the company also offer voyages north to Orkney, Shetland and Norway. She sails mainly from her home port of Oban and is claimed to offer 'the unrivalled comfort and refined service of a floating country house with a minimum of 50 guests in the tradition of the halcyon days of cruising'. The *Hebridean Princess* offers cruises that include meals and drinks, guides and guest speakers, shore visits, use of bicycles, Internet, transfer and car parking, port taxes and gratuities. The ship is also available for private charters. The company launched the *Royal Crown* in 2012, offering Rhine and Danube river cruises. The number of sailings offered on *Royal Crown* was increased in 2013 to include the Main and the Rhine-Main-Danube Canal, in addition to the Rhine and Danube rivers.

Saga acquired the *Sagafjord* in 1996, and renamed her *Saga Rose*. She was able to carry 587 passengers, and had sixty-three single cabins and 350 crew. Saga's philosophy is to provide cruises for people over fifty years of age, and offer a wide variety of holidays from the United Kingdom, including world cruises. *Sagafjord*'s sister ship was purchased from Cunard in 2005, becoming *Saga Ruby*, with *Saga Rose* being scrapped in 2010. The company now operate *Saga Sapphire* and *Quest for Adventure*, as *Saga Ruby* was retired early in 2014.

Carnival Cruise Lines was the idea of Ted Arison in 1972 with 'a boatload of vision, a single second-hand ship and just enough fuel to make the one-way trip from Miami to San Juan'. *Empress of Canada* was purchased from Canadian Pacific and renamed *Mardi Gras*. Unfortunately, she ran aground on a sandbar outside the Port of Miami, but she was successfully refloated and continued in service. *Empress of Britain* was acquired in 1975, becoming *Carnivale*; *SA Vaal* was purchased three years later and renamed *Festival*, following a $30-million refit.

Their first new ship, *Tropicale*, made her debut in 1982, with Carnival becoming the first cruise line to advertise on network television two years later. *Holiday* followed in 1985, *Jubilee* the following year and *Celebration* in 1987. That year Carnival earned the distinction of 'Most Popular Cruise Line in the World', carrying more passengers than any other. In 1987, it offered 20 per cent of its stock to the public, raising approximately $400 million to fuel expansion programmes. It was then able to acquire the Holland America Line, including Windstar Cruises in 1987, Holland America Tours two years later, and the Seabourn Cruise Line in 1992.

The first 'Fantasy class' vessel, *Fantasy*, came in to service in 1990 and was placed on the three- and four-day Bahama cruise programme from Miami. *Ecstasy* was introduced in 1991, *Sensation* in 1993 and *Fascination* the following year, when the parent company was renamed Carnival Corporation. *Imagination* was introduced in 1995 and the sixth 'Fantasy class', *Inspiration*, in 1996. *Carnival Destiny*, the first passenger vessel to exceed 100,000 tons, also joined the fleet in 1996.

The programme of expansion continued when the Cunard Line was taken over in 1998, and Costa Line in 2000. The seventh 'Fantasy class', *Elation*, and eighth and last in the series, *Paradise*, entered service in 1998. The following year, Carnival's second 'Destiny class', *Carnival Triumph*, made her debut, and *Carnival Victory* was launched in 2000. In 2001, *Carnival Spirit*, the 'Fun Ship', was positioned in the Alaska and Hawaii market. *Carnival Pride* was also delivered in 2001.

Carnival Legend debuted in August 2002, and the *Carnival Conquest* began year-round seven-day cruises in December that year. *Carnival Glory* was introduced in 2003, *Carnival Miracle* in 2004, *Carnival Valor* in 2004 and *Carnival Liberty* in 2005. *Carnival Freedom* followed in 2007, *Carnival Splendour* in 2008 and the largest 'Fun Ship', *Carnival Dream*, in 2009. A second 'Dream Class', *Carnival Magic*, followed in 2011, with a third, *Carnival Breeze*, in 2012.

Ocean Monarch in the River Fal. She was launched on 27 July 1950 at the Vickers Armstrong yard on the Tyne, and sailed on her maiden voyage from London to New York on 18 April the following year. Her first voyage from New York to Bermuda commenced on 3 May, carrying 440 first-class passengers. She was given a major refit in 1961 when her tonnage was relisted as 13,581 gross registered tons. *Ocean Monarch* remained on that service, with occasional calls at Nassau, until 1966 when she was withdrawn and laid up on the River Fal.

She was sold to the Bulgarian Shipping Company in 1967 to be used as a cruise ship in the Mediterranean and Black Sea, and renamed *Varna*. She also operated to the St Lawrence between 1970 and 1972, with cruises from Montreal and from Nice in 1973. Following the sudden increase in oil prices, she was laid up for several years, and in 1979 she was refitted for use in the Mediterranean and renamed *Riviera*; however, this service never materialised, and it was rumoured that she was to be chartered by World Cruise Lines for the New York–Bermuda service.

It was also thought that she would be renamed *Venus* for cruising from New York and Florida but she was, in fact, renamed *Reina Del Mar* in 1981 for a proposed service to Scandinavia and the North Cape in the summer, and the Mediterranean in the winter. However, while undergoing a refit on 28 May 1981 she suffered a serious fire at Perama; she later capsized and was declared a total loss.

Varna.

Queen of Bermuda and her sister, *Monarch of Bermuda*, left New York at 15.00 on Saturdays, arriving at St Georges, Bermuda, at 09.00 on Mondays, and passengers were tendered to Hamilton. They departed on Wednesday, arriving at New York at 08.00 on Friday. In 1939 *Monarch of Bermuda* became a troop carrier, and operated to Norway, Italy, Portugal and North Africa, and by the end of hostilities she had transported 164,840 personnel and steamed 450,512 miles. On 24 March 1947, while being converted back to a passenger vessel, she was almost destroyed by fire. She was purchased by the Ministry of Transport and rebuilt by J. I. Thornycroft as an emigrant carrier and renamed *New Australia*. She sailed on her first voyage from Southampton to Sydney on 15 August 1950, managed by Shaw Savill & Albion. In 1953 she carried troops to Korea, and was sold to the Greek Line in 1958, refitted by Bloom & Voss at Hamburg and renamed *Arkadia*. Following this refit she was able to accommodate 150 first-class and 1,150 tourist-class passengers, sailing on her first voyage for the line from Bremerhaven to Quebec and Montreal on 22 May 1958. She continued in service until she was sold to ship-breakers at Valencia, where she arrived on 18 December 1966. Her sister *Queen of Bermuda* was launched at Vickers Armstrong on 1 September 1932 and sailed on her maiden voyage from Liverpool to New York on 21 February 1933. She then joined the *Monarch of Bermuda* on the New York–Bermuda service. In 1937 her registry was also changed from Bermuda to London, and in 1939 she was taken over and converted into an armed merchant cruiser.

Queen of Bermuda was fitted with seven 6-inch guns and anti-aircraft weapons, and in 1940 her third funnel was removed. She was converted to a troopship in 1943, and carried over 97,000 troops during the remainder of the war. In 1947 she was refitted for peacetime use; she had her third funnel replaced, and three new boilers replaced the original eight.

She was sent to Harland & Wolff at Belfast for her annual overhaul in 1961, and was rebuilt with one funnel. Following successful sea trials on 23 February 1962, she returned to the New York–Bermuda service. On 23 November 1963 she returned to Cammell Laird for her annual refit, which took five weeks to complete. Furness Withy closed the passenger service in 1966, and *Queen of Bermuda* was sold to Shipbreaking Industries Limited to be broken up at Faslane, where she arrived on 6 December.

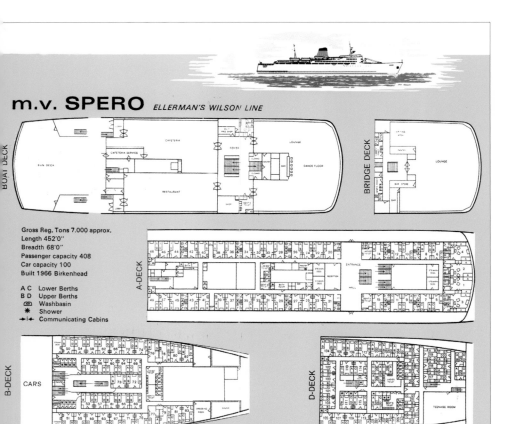

m.v. SPERO ELLERMAN'S WILSON LINE

BOAT DECK

SUN DECK · CAFETERIA · CAFETERIA SERVICE · FOYER · LOUNGE · DANCE FLOOR · BAR · RESTAURANT · SHOP

BRIDGE DECK

LOUNGE · BAR STORE · BAR

Gross Reg. Tons 7.000 approx.
Length 452'0"
Breadth 68'0"
Passenger capacity 408
Car capacity 100
Built 1966 Birkenhead

A C Lower Berths
B D Upper Berths
☐ Washbasin
✳ Shower
◀━▶ Communicating Cabins

A-DECK

ENTRANCE · RECEPTION · HALL

B-DECK

CARS

D-DECK

TEENAGE ROOM

Ellerman Wilson Line *Spero*. *Spero* was built by Cammell Laird for the Hull–Gothenburg service of England Sweden Line, operated by Wilson Line, Svea Line of Stockholm, and Swedish Lloyd of Gothenburg. She was Ellerman Wilson Line's contribution to the new service, and was designed to carry 408 passengers, 100 cars and 100 containers or trailers. The three ships were designed to be capable of carrying over 3,500 passengers, 1,000 cars and over 13,500 tons of cargo each week.

She was the first ship to be fitted with Sperry 'Gyrofin' twin-folding stabilisers, and her hydraulically operated stern door was the largest ever fitted to a British ship of this type. Her four diesel engines were designed to be controlled either from the bridge or from a soundproofed machinery control room. She was also fitted with a close circuit television system that was used as a navigation aid for docking.

When *Spero* was launched from the same slipway as *Mauretania* and HMS *Ark Royal*, she was already fitted with her four diesel engines and generating plant, gearbox, various auxiliary machinery, main switchboard, deck cranes, hatch covers and galley equipment. Some cabins were finished, and the trunking from the engine room was in place for her funnel, which was the third-largest ever built at the yard. Two Mirrless diesel engines, developing 2,730 bhp, powered her, which drove the twin screws.

Following the launch, Colonel Bayley, managing director of Ellerman's Wilson Line, said that each of the three companies involved in the service had over 100 years' experience in providing regular services across the North Sea. The England Sweden Line introduced radical modifications in cargo-handling techniques, as the ships offered facilities to importers and exporters for all kind of freight, whether unitised by means of containers, trailers, pallets, flats or lorries.

The Marine Superintendent of Ellerman's Wilson Line, Captain R. Tanton OBE stressed that the design of *Spero* was extremely complex because of the necessity to build a ship to carry passengers, cars and unitised cargo. Mr R. W. Johnson, chairman of Cammell Laird, praised the cooperation management had experienced from the unions, and said that the yard was very competitive following a streamlining of costs, even against Japanese builders, who were experiencing a noticeable dip in profits as their costs were mounting, both for material and labour, and they were having to revise their ideas on prices.

In 1972 *Spero* operated briefly to Zeebrugge, and was sold and renamed *Sappho* by her new Greek owners. In 2002 she was sold to Lacerta Shipping (Tanzania) Limited, becoming *Santorini 3*, and was broken up at Alang in 2004.

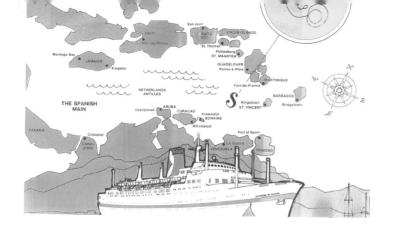

Canadian Pacific *Empress of Canada* Caribbean cruises.

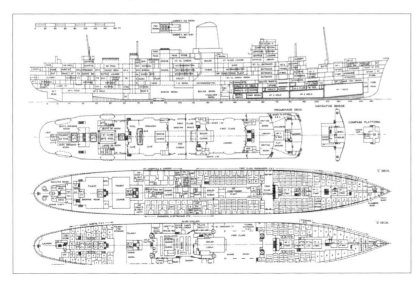

Plan of *Arcadia*.

Orcades.

P&O Cruises, 1971.

Top left: Queen Elizabeth.

Top right: Queen Elizabeth pool.

Left: Queen Elizabeth restaurant.

Top left: Queen Elizabeth cinema.

Top right: Queen Elizabeth main lounge.

Right: Seawise University on fire at Hong Kong.

S.S. 'REINA DEL MAR' (20,750 tons)

To ALLAN
FROM EDDIE
"BON VOYAGE"

Farewell Voyage

from CAPE TOWN
To
MADEIRA and SOUTHAMPTON
17th March—1st April 1975

UNION-CASTLE

Reina del Mar Farewell Voyage Menu.

Reina del Mar leaves Liverpool on a TSA cruise.

Cunard Ambassador was launched on 16 March 1972, and sailed on her maiden voyage from Southampton to San Juan on 23 October that year. On 12 September 1974, on a light voyage from Port Everglades to New Orleans, she suffered a serious engine room fire and was abandoned near Key West, and was later towed into that port. It was decided that it was uneconomic to repair her, and she was sold in 1975, rebuilt as a livestock carrier and renamed *Linda Clausen*, for the Australia–Persian Gulf service. She became *Procyn* in 1980, *Raslan* in 1983, and was broken up at Kaohsiung the following year.

Holidays in America

Fares from £195 to £503

Queen Elizabeth 2

France

CUNARD/FRENCH LINE

Entente Cordiale Cunard/French Line Holidays in America by *Queen Elizabeth 2* and *France* in 1972.

COAST LINES

AHOY!

1967

COASTAL CRUISES

Coast Line Coastal Cruises, 1967.

Hibernian Coast.

Centaur was launched on 20 June 1963 by Mrs D. Bland, wife of the prime minister of Western Australia, and completed at a cost of £2½ million. She left Liverpool on her maiden voyage to Sydney on 20 January 1964, and operated on a three-weekly service from Fremantle and Western Australian ports to Singapore, with accommodation for 190 first-class passengers, refrigerated cargo, 4,500 sheep and 700 cattle. She took her first sailing on charter to the Australian Chambers of Trade mission. She was transferred to the China Mutual Steam Navigation Company in 1967, and in 1973 to the ownership of Eastern Fleets Limited section, managed by the Straits Steam Ship Co. Ltd of Singapore. In 1978 she was owned by Blue Funnel (S.E.A.) Pte. Limited of Singapore, and took her final sailing from Fremantle on 15 September 1981. The following year she was chartered to the St Helena Shipping Company to replace their ship, which had been chartered for Falkland Islands service. She arrived at Avonmouth on 29 November 1982, and it was hoped that she would find a new home on the St Helena service. However, she was in poor condition and suffering machinery problems, and sailed from Avonmouth to Singapore via Cape Town and Fremantle on 18 October 1983. Her funnel was repainted in Blue Funnel colours at Cape Town and she was laid up when she arrived at Singapore. In 1985 she was sold to Shanghai Hai Xing Shipping Company and became *Hai Long* and *Hai Da* the following year. She survived until 1995 ,when she was scrapped at Xinhui, Guangdong, China.

Carnival Corporation is the larger of the two holding companies, with Micky Arison, the founder's son, holding 47 per cent of the company. Pacific Interstate Airlines was bought in 1988, and was renamed Carnival Air Lines the following year, operating between San Juan, Orlando, Miami and Islip. The company was purchased by Pan American Airlines in 1997, but soon suffered financial difficulties when it filed for bankruptcy, and ceased operations in 1998.

Carnival plc is the United Kingdom-listed company of the Carnival Group, and was formed as a result of the merger between the Carnival Corporation and P&O Princess Cruises in 2003. P&O Princess remained a separate company, and was subsequently relisted as Carnival plc. P&O Princess Cruises owned P&O Cruises, P&O Cruises Australia, Princess Cruises, Ocean Village and AIDA Cruises. Carnival UK also took control of the Cunard Line.

Windstar was sold to Ambassadors International Cruise Group and Swan Hellenic to Lord Sterling in 2007.

Carnival comprises the following:–

AIDA Cruises, Germany
Carnival Cruise Lines, United States
Costa Cruises, Italy
Cunard Line, United Kingdom
Holland America Line, United States
Ibero Cruises, Spain
P&O Cruises, United Kingdom
P&O Cruises Australia, Australia
Princess Cruises, United States
Seabourn Cruise Line, United States

The company also operated the Ocean Village Company from 2003 to 2010.

In 2011 the combined brands of Carnival Corporation controlled a 49.2 per cent share of the total worldwide cruise market. Together, these brands operate 100 ships, totalling 203,000 lower berths, with nine new ships scheduled to be delivered between March 2013 and March 2016. Carnival Corporation & plc also operates Holland America Princess Alaska Tours, the leading tour company in Alaska and the Canadian Yukon, which complements the Alaska cruise operations. The company is traded on both the New York and London Stock Exchanges; Carnival Corporation & plc is the only group in the world to be included in both the S&P 500 and the FTSE 100 indices.

	Passenger Capacity	Number of ships
P&O Cruises (UK)	14,636	7
Cunard	6,672	3

Cruise Brands	Ship's Fiscal Year	Scheduled for Funding Amount (in millions)
North America		
Princess		
Royal Princess	2013	$523
Regal Princess	2014	523
P&O Cruises (UK)		
Newbuild *Britannia*	2015	539

Embarking and Disembarking Passengers at UK Ports, 2003–2009

Passengers (000s)	2003	2004	2005	2006	2007	2008	2009	% Change (2003–2009)
Disembarkations	377	430	497	579	584	707	740	+96%
Embarkations	375	428	503	576	591	714	733	+95%
Annual % Increase Embarkations	21	14	18	15	3	21	3	
UK Passenger Embarkations	281	316	403	451	460	557	5	94
Overseas Passenger Embarkations	94	112	100	125	124	157	139	
% Overseas Embarkations	25	26	20	22	21	22	19	

Source: IRN Research – Cruise Port Statistics, 2009

Port of Call Passengers by Region, 2003–2009

Pax (000s)	2003	2004	2005	2006	2007	2008	2009	% Change 2003–2009
Scotland	111.1	119.8	147.7	175.7	165.0	182.7	218.9	+97%
North Country	11.9	8.4	5.3	4.5	8.5	31.9	32.0	+169%
East of England	6.1	4.6	3.8	16.1	5.3	4.6	2.0	-67%
South of England	86.5	157.2	124.7	152.8	141.3	147.8	143.8	+66%
Wales	8.3	8.1	15.4	11.0	14.7	7.3	5.6	-23%
Northern Ireland	7.6	26.5	25.4	21.9	30.1	45.2	45.6	+500%
TOTAL	231.4	324	322.2	382.0	365.0	419.6	448.0	+94%

Source: IRN Research – Cruise Port Statistics

2013 Share of World Wide Passengers

Parent	Brand	
Carnival	Seabourn	0.3%
	Princess	6.1%
	P&O Cruises Australia	1.6%
	P&O Cruises	1.7%
	Ibero Cruises	1.1%
	Holland America	3.3%
	Cunard	0.7%
	Costa Cruises	7.7%
	Carnival	21.2%
	Aida	4.6%
	Total	48.4%
RCL	Royal Caribbean	16.4%
	Pullmantur	1.9%
	Celebrity	4.4%
	CDF	0.4%
	Azamara	0.2%
	Total	23.3%
Others	Windstar	0.1%
	Voyages to Antiquity	0.0%
	Thomson Cruises	1.4%
	TUI Cruises	0.8%
	Swan Hellenic	0.0%
	Star Cruises	1.4%
	Star Clippers	0.1%
	Silversea	0.4%
	SeaDream Yacht Club	0.0%

	Saga Cruises	0.4%
	Regent Seven Seas	0.3%
	Ponant Yacht Cruises	0.2%
	Phoenix Reisen	0.5%
	Pearl Seas Cruises	0.0%
	Paul Gauguin	0.1%
	Orient Expedition Cruises	0.0%
	Oceania Cruises	0.5%
	Ocean Star Cruises	0.2%
	Norwegian	7.6%
	MSC Cruises	7.0%
	Louis Cruises	0.9%
	Lindblad Expeditions	0.1%
	Hurtigruten	1.3%
	Hebridean Island Cruises	0.0%
	Hapag-Lloyd	0.2%
	Fred Olsen	0.4%
	Disney	2.5%
	Discovery World Cruises	0.1%
	Crystal	0.3%
	Cruise & Maritime Voyages	0.3%
	Classic International Cruises	0.4%
	Celebration Cruise Line	0.2%
	Blount Small Ship Adventures	0.0%
	American Cruise Lines	0.1%
	All Leisure Holidays	0.3%
	Total	28.3%
	Grand Total	100.0%

Ellerman Line's *City of Durban* loading at London Docks. She was built by Vickers Armstrong & Company on the Tyne in 1954 for the company's London–Las Palmas, Cape Town, Port Elizabeth, East London, Durban, Lourenço Marques and Beira passenger and cargo services. She was sold to Michail A. Karageorgis Lines Corporation, Panama, in 1971, becoming *Mediterranean Dolphin*, and was laid up at Perama. On 30 March 1974 she arrived at Kaohsiung to be broken up.

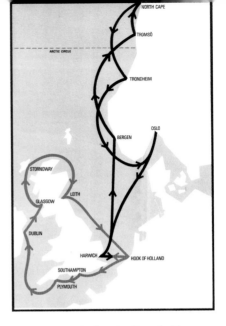

Above left: Avalon cruise map, 1970. *Avalon* was built for the British Transport Commission by Alexander Stephens & Sons in 1963, for the Harwich–Hook of Holland route. She cost £2 million to build, and replaced *Duke of York* on the route. She had also been designed to undertake off-season cruising, and was fitted with berths for 320 in one class. Her classification certificate allowed her to cruise as far as Gibraltar, but this was later extended to Tangier. She sailed regularly to Oporto and Lisbon, and in 1966 she was chartered by Ellerman Wilson Line because of the late delivery of their new vessel, *Spero*. On 26 October 1967 she was chartered by the Gulf Oil Corporation for a week to convey guests to the opening of the Bantry Bay refinery and to witness the arrival of Gulf Oil's super-tanker *Universe Ireland*. She also cruised to Rotterdam. In 1974 she was converted to a car-ferry, and her lower accommodation was removed. The following year she replaced *Caledonian Princess* on the Fishguard–Rosslare route. *Avalon* was also used on other British Rail routes, and was replaced by *Stena Normandica* in 1979. The following year she was laid up at Barrow and was sold to Cyprus interests and renamed *Valon*. On 22 January 1981 she arrived at Gadani Beach to be broken up.

Above right: Midnight Sun and Round Britain Cruises by *Avalon*, 1970.

Right: Elders & Fyffes Line, 1970. The line operated a service from Southampton to Bermuda, Jamaica, Antigua and Trinidad, and was formed in 1901 to transport bananas from the West Indies to the United Kingdom. Elders & Fyffes continued in this trade until their withdrawal from shipping in the early 1970s, and the last two ships they owned were the *Golfito* and *Camito*. Gordon Holman, author of *The Little Ships*, described these two ships as being

neither too large nor too small when a double crossing of the Atlantic is involved. A floating island of this size, with comfortable accommodation for slightly less than 100 passengers, must have the personal touch. The white painted liners belonging to Fyffes Line, a name which should indicate in which direction you will be going to get away from it all. In 10 days you are in the Caribbean, with Jamaica as your turnaround point after a brief stay.

Below: Camito.

FLEET		Gross	Passengers
Ship		Tonnage	Carried
s.s. CAMITO	..	8,500	96
s.s. GOLFITO	..	8,500	94
s.s. CHANGUINOLA		6,000	12
s.s. CHICANOA	..	6,000	12
s.s. CHUSCAL		6,000	12
s.s. MATINA		6,500	6
s.s. MORANT	..	6,500	6
s.s. PACUARE		5,000	10
s.s. RIO COBRE		6,500	12
s.s. ROATAN	..	6,500	12
s.s. TELDE	..	6,500	5
s.s. TILAPA	..	6,500	5
s.s. TUCURINCA	..	6,500	5
s.s. TURRIALBA	..	6,500	5
Building			
s.s. MOTAGUA	..	6,500	6

GENERAL PASSENGER AGENTS

JAMAICA
United Fruit Jamaica Company, P.O. Box 282, Kingston
(*Cable Address:* UNIFRUITCO)

TRINIDAD
Geo. F. Huggins & Co. Ltd., P.O. Box 179, Port of Spain
(*Cable Address:* HUGGINS)

BERMUDA
Wm. E. Meyer & Co. Ltd., St. George's
(*Cable Address:* DARMEY)

ANTIGUA
Geo. W. Bennett, Bryson & Co. Ltd., P.O. Box 162,
St. John's
(*Cable Address:* BENNETT)

Fyffes
LINE

**ANTIGUA
TRINIDAD
JAMAICA
BERMUDA**

**Sailing List &
Passage Tariff No.12**

ISSUED SUBJECT TO ALTERATION OR CANCELLATION WITHOUT NOTICE

JANUARY 1970

Empress of England to *Ocean Monarch*. Vickers Armstrong Limited at Walker on Tyne built *Ocean Monarch* as *Empress of England* for the Canadian Pacific Steamships Company, and she was launched by Lady Eden, wife of the British prime minister, on 9 May 1956. She was an almost identical sister ship to the *Empress of Britain*, which was built by the Fairfield Shipbuilding & Engineering Company, Govan, the previous year.

The *Empress of England* sailed on her maiden voyage from Liverpool to Quebec and Montreal on 18 April 1957, when she replaced the *Empress of Scotland*. In 1962 she broke adrift in Gladstone Dock at Liverpool, and collided with the *Hindustan*. Both ships were damaged in the collision. In 1963 she was chartered by the Travel Savings Association and sailed on her first cruise for them on 28 October from Cape Town. In 1964 she returned to the Canadian Pacific Steamships route from Liverpool to Montreal, which she maintained until 1970 when she was sold to the Shaw Savill & Albion Line and renamed *Ocean Monarch*.

She made one round sailing from Liverpool to Southampton and Australia, then returned to Cammell Laird for refitting into a one-class liner. She sailed from Merseyside on 17 September 1971, but as she was delayed due to industrial action, the Line was forced to cancel twelve cruises she was due to make that summer. She made only one Mediterranean cruise that year, leaving Southampton on 16 October.

On 5 November she left Southampton for Barbados, Curaçao, Panama, Acapulco, Los Angeles, Vancouver, Honolulu, Tokeleu Island, Fiji, and Auckland. She was employed on a cruising programme out of Sydney in 1973, but as she suffered serious mechanical problems in 1974 she returned to Britain and completed a series of cruises from Southampton. *Ocean Monarch* arrived at Southampton on her last cruise on 5 June 1975 and sailed to the ship-breakers at Kaohsiung the following week.

BLUE STAR LINE

LISBON & SOUTH AMERICA

CARRYING H.M. MAILS

s.s. "PARAGUAY STAR"

FOR

LISBON Due 24th Dec.	**TENERIFFE** Due 27th Dec.
RIO DE JANEIRO Due 5th Jan.	**SANTOS** Due 7th Jan.
MONTEVIDEO Due 10th Jan.	**BUENOS AIRES** Due 11th Jan.

Receiving Cargo at

No. 16 SHED, ROYAL ALBERT DOCK, LONDON

From 13th Dec. until 18th Dec.

REFRIGERATED SPACE AVAILABLE

CARGO FOR BRAZIL AND URUGUAY MUST BE SPECIALLY BOOKED BEFORE DELIVERY

All Bills of Lading **MUST** be lodged by closing date

NEXT SAILING

m.v. "IBERIA STAR" closing for cargo 1st Jan.

INSURANCE EFFECTED AT COMPETITIVE RATES

For further particulars, rates of freight, etc., apply:—

BLUE STAR LINE
LTD.

ALBION HOUSE, LEADENHALL STREET, LONDON, E.C.3
TELEPHONE: ROYAL 4567

BIRMINGHAM 6 Victoria Square **MANCHESTER** 556 Royal Exchange
GLASGOW 93 Hope Street

Passenger Office: 3 LOWER REGENT STREET LONDON, S.W.1 (For other Agents see overleaf)

This is a 2 bedded cabin on Northern Star, available with private facilities.

This is a 2 bedded cabin on Ocean Monarch, available with private facilities, on A Deck.

This is a 2 berth cabin on Northern Star, available with or without private facilities. Sometimes these are sold as single cabins, when the upper berth is folded back.

This is a 2 berth cabin on Ocean Monarch, available with or without private facilities. Sometimes these are sold as single cabins, when the upper berth is folded back.

This is a 4 berth cabin on Northern Star. 6 berth cabins are similar in lay-out and style. 4 berth cabins may be sold as 2 bedded cabins, when the upper berths are folded back.

This is a 4 berth cabin on Ocean Monarch, available with or without private facilities. 4 berth cabins may be sold as 2 bedded cabins, when the upper berths are folded back.

Blue Star Line sailing list. The Blue Star vessels on the Australasian and North Pacific Coast trades were essentially cargo vessels, but were also fitted with accommodation for a small number of passengers. The public rooms comprised a Dining Saloon and Lounge, and there was a Card Room on some of the vessels. All of the accommodation was situated on the Bridge Deck and on the majority of vessels there were large windows with a clear, unobstructed view out to sea. Ample deck space for recreation was provided, combined with a high standard of cuisine and service, for which the ships had established a high reputation. Return fares for the voyage from London to Montevideo and Buenos Aires in 1961 ranged from £342 per person in a single room without bath, to £407 in a double room with bath. It was also possible to travel as far as Rio de Janeiro, and stay there for three days, then return to London, giving a voyage of about five weeks.

JAN— —DEC 1970

BLUE STAR LINE

SOUTH AMERICAN SERVICE

CHIEF PASSENGER OFFICE
LOWER REGENT STREET LONDON S.W.I

Above: Uruguay Star was built by Cammell Laird at Birkenhead in 1947 and was similar to *Argentina Star*, *Brasil Star* and *Paraguay Star*. They were built for the Blue Star Line's service from London to Lisbon, Tenerife, Rio de Janeiro, Santos, Montevideo and Buenos Aires and carried sixty first-class passengers in single and double cabins on the bridge deck. She was sold in 1972 to be broken up at Kaohsiung, where she arrived on 25 August that year. *Argentina Star* and *Brasil Star* were also broken up at Kaohsiung in October and December 1972, respectively. *Paraguay Star* had suffered a serious fire on 12 August 1969 while discharging in the Royal Victoria Dock, London, and had been declared beyond economic repair, and broken up at Hamburg.

Left: Blue Star Line 1970.

Geest Line has operated cargo and passenger services between the United Kingdom and the Caribbean for over fifty years, and now carries more cargo between Europe and the Windward and Leeward Islands than any other shipping line. Bananas were shipped eastbound, and general cargo was carried to the islands. According to surveys the Geest Line has the highest schedule reliability for round trip crossings, and the shortest transit times to the port of call in the Caribbean. The perishable nature of the cargo dictates that the ships must arrive and depart on time, enabling the company to offer a precise, fixed-day service, which allows shippers to be certain that the goods will arrive on time.

The new *Reina del Mar* in the Panama Canal in 1956.

COOKS OFFICE- YOUR BEST PORT-OF-CALL ON THE "REINA DEL MAR"

Ports-of-call are always among the high-spots of any cruise and as they appear one-by-one over the horizon, the prospect of a spell ashore looms equally large. Always on call is the Reina del Mar's own Cooks office with a programme of escorted shore excursions designed to make your cruise all the more enjoyable and memorable.

Call into Cooks and make yourself known. You will find the staff friendly . . . *helpful*. But then of course being Cooks trained they know the cruise business from A to Z and all ports in between!

Always carry Cooks Travel Cheques

COOKS
world-wide travel service

Cook's *Reina del Mar* advertisement, 1971.

Cruise down to Tangier

the new 11,500 ton cruise liner car ferry EAGLE

restaurant.

A de luxe two berth cabin.

The games deck.

...th or without your car, a full length holiday.

...e is more in the cruise liner class
...capacity for 750 passengers.
...e's a swimming pool, a games
..., two restaurants, four bars, a night
...cinema shows, an arcade of duty-
...shops and facilities for children.
...here's more to *Eagle* than just
...e liner fun. There's cruise liner
...fort.

...eautifully designed, furnished and
...eted throughout, *Eagle* has really
...d accommodation. Twin-bedded
...s and de luxe cabins. Two, three
...our berth cabins, each with its
...w.c. wash basin and shower. And
...t important, *Eagle*
...stabilized.

The panoramic bar.

If you want to get more out of your
holiday in Morocco, *Eagle* is the
answer. A three day cruise each way.
A fortnight or more on
land. A relaxing holiday,
from the first day
to the last.

The swimming pool, with its patio bar.

The shopping centre.

Azur, ex-*Eagle*.

Left: Cruise down to Tangier on *Eagle*. *Eagle* was owned by the General Steam Navigation Company's Southern Ferries, and was built in 1971 for a service to Spain, Portugal and Morocco. She was specifically built for the service, which initially proved popular and successful. However, after operating for only five seasons and following political unrest in Portugal, it was decided to sell the vessel to Compagnie de Paquebots in October 1976. She was renamed *Azur*, later *The Azur* and converted to a cruise ship in 1981, with additional cabins fitted to her former garage deck. She was chartered to Chandris from 1987 to 1994 and was later operating for Festival Cruises. Since 2004 she has been operating for Mano Maritime of Israel as *Royal Iris*, with *Golden Iris*, previously *Cunard Princess* and *Rhapsody*.

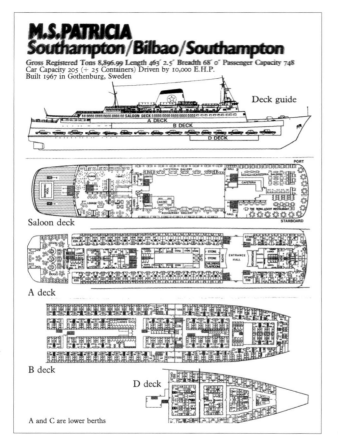

M.S.PATRICIA
Southampton/Bilbao/Southampton

Gross Registered Tons 8,896.99 Length 463′ 2.5″ Breadth 68′ 0″ Passenger Capacity 748
Car Capacity 205 (+ 25 Containers) Driven by 10,000 E.H.P.
Built 1967 in Gothenburg, Sweden

Deck guide

Saloon deck

A deck

B deck

D deck

A and C are lower berths

Patricia plan.

Swedish Lloyd and Southern Ferries Motoring Holidays, 1971/72. Both companies operated a joint service from Southampton to Spain, Portugal and Morroco in 1971–72.

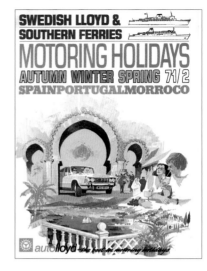

Cunard's Caribbean Fly/Cruises, 1973. The holiday included the BOAC flight from the United Kingdom to St Lucia, and a stay in a hotel for five days prior to boarding the *Cunard Adventurer* for a cruise in the Caribbean. The package then included another period in a hotel before leaving for the flight back to London Heathrow.

Cunard's other world.

Caribbean Fly-cruises

Fly BOAC to the Caribbean any Friday through summer and autumn. Cruise for a week on the new Cunard Adventurer. Before and after, stay at Hotel La Toc, the Cunard Group's latest luxury hotel on St Lucia.

Day 1 Leave London by BOAC scheduled jet direct to St Lucia. Transfer to Hotel La Toc.

Days 2–7 Five lazy days in your own secluded valley on this romantic island. The brand-new hotel has superb views over one of the finest beaches in St Lucia, all of which is exclusively yours. Two restaurants, bars, a swimming pool – naturally, three floodlit tennis courts (with a resident professional), a 9-hole golf course are all at your command, plus the usual water sports.

Day 7 Transfer to Cunard Adventurer in the afternoon, a short drive away in Castries harbour. The latest addition to the Cunard fleet, she's fully air-conditioned and stabilised, and more like a graceful yacht. All cabins are twin-bedded or singles – all have private bath or shower. Sail on your seven-day cruise to the most exciting ports-of-call in the Caribbean – this is the outline itinerary:

Day 8 St Thomas	1030 – 2359
Day 9 San Juan	0800 – 2359
Day 10 At sea	
Day 11 Curacao	0800 – 2200
Day 12 La Guaira, Caracas	0800 – 1900
Day 13 Grenada	1300 – 2000

Days 14–16 Back to St Lucia and Hotel La Toc. The final days to soak up the sun, laze on the beach, go sightseeing or try water-skiing, wine, dine and dance luxury style. Evening on your last day comes all too soon – time to leave for your BOAC scheduled flight home.

Day 17 Arrive after breakfast at London (Heathrow).

The price includes round trip on BOAC scheduled St Lucia; transfers between hotel and airport: bed, breakfast and dinner at hotel: 7-day cruise on Cunard Adventurer including all meals and entertainment on board.

Gratuities are not included. At the hotel a 10% service charge will be added to your bill in lieu; on Cunard Adventurer gratuities are at your own discretion.

16 days (15-nights) holiday from £229

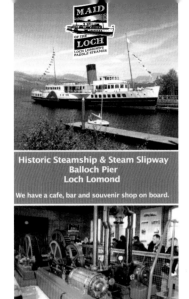

Historic Steamship & Steam Slipway
Balloch Pier
Loch Lomond
We have a cafe, bar and souvenir shop on board.

Right: Loch Lomond Steamer services, 1957.

Far right: Cunard Adventurer.

Maid of the Loch was launched on 5 March 1953 for the passenger and cruise services on Loch Lomond. She was used to operate cruises on the loch, and was in service until August 1981. *Maid of the Loch* sailed from Balloch Pier and sailed initially to Ardlui, and later to Inversnaid. In 1969 she became the responsibility of the Scottish Transport Group and later Caledonia MacBrayne. She was purchased by Dumbarton District Council in 1992 and three years later the Loch Lomond Steamship Company were given responsibility for restoring the vessel. A Heritage Lottery Fund grant was obtained to lift the steamer out of the water in 2006, and following the work of the volunteers she is now open to the public as a static example of a passenger paddle steamer. An appeal for £3.3 million was launched in early 2013 to bring the ship back into steam, and in addition a further £1.6 million is required for supporting infrastructure, which will create a visitor centre at Balloch pier and allow repair work to be carried out on some of the other piers on Loch Lomond.

Victoria was built as the Union Castle passenger vessel *Dunnottar Castle* by Harland & Wolff at Belfast in 1936. She was converted to an Armed Merchant Cruiser in 1939 and a troopship in 1942. Returning to peacetime duties in 1949, she was sold to the Incres Line in 1958 and renamed *Victoria*. Following a major overhaul, and re-engined the following year at Rotterdam, she was advertised to operate Mediterranean cruises for her new owner. She became *The Victoria* in 1976, when operating for Chandris Lines, and *Princess Victoria* in 1993, when owned by Louis Cruise Lines. She was laid up at Perama and operated short cruises from Cyprus; she was used as a floating hotel for Expo '98 and for the G8 summit in Genoa in 2001. Prior to being broken up in India in 2004, it was claimed that she was the oldest passenger liner operating anywhere in the world.

Amerikanis was originally the Union Castle passenger liner *Kenya Castle*.

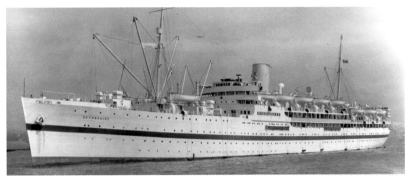

Daphne was built as the cargo vessel *Port Sydney* in 1955 and was sold in 1972, becoming *Akrotiri Express*, operating for Chion Shipping Company, Piraeus. However, in 1974 she was converted to a passenger/cruise ship and renamed *Daphne*. In the following years she was operated by Delian Athina Cruises and Flotta Lauro, and in 1979 she was placed on charter to Coast Cruises for five years. At the end of the charter she was purchased by Costa. She has since been operating as *Switzerland*, *Ocean Odyssey*, *Ocean Monarch* and *Princess Daphne*. Her sister, *Port Melbourne*, was also converted to a cruise ship and has operated as *Therisos Express*, *Danae*, *Anar*, *Starlight Princess*, *Baltica*, and *Princess Danae*.

Devonshire was built as a troop transport and spent the Second World War transporting troops to the Far East, Australia, South Africa and the Mediterranean. She was converted to a Landing Ship for the Infantry in 1943 and took part in the invasion of Sicily. In 1953 she was refitted and chartered to the Sea Transport Division of the Ministry of Transport, and her base was transferred from Liverpool to Southampton. She was sold to the British India Line in 1962 and converted to an educational cruise ship, renamed *Devonia* to operate with *Dunera*. In this role she carried 190 first-class, 96 second-class passengers and 830 students, in dormitories. She continued in this role as an educational cruise vessel until 1967 when she was sold and broken up at Le Spezia.

The latest figures for the numbers of United Kingdom cruise passengers show an 11 per cent growth year on year, and more people visited the country through the fifty-two cruise ports than ever before. Cruise ships brought a record number of 723,000 passengers to the United Kingdom in 2012, a 10 per cent increase. In 2010 there were 1.6 million passengers on cruises beginning or ending at United Kingdom ports, and passenger numbers on cruise journeys rose by 16 per cent between 2009 and 2010. Cruise journeys have risen year on year since 1999. Consequently, the United Kingdom is becoming a very popular cruise destination, and cruising is becoming a favoured option for people who live in the British Isles. Its popularity may be due to the variety of experiences and attractions available such as the countryside, historic towns and cities, castles and its coastal villages.

In 1965 Elizabeth Nicholas, travel correspondent for the *Sunday Times*, wrote,

Cruising can be all things to all men, the variety is tremendous, the range no less enormous. You pays your money and takes your choice; it is as easy as that. You may book for a long luxurious Caribbean and Pacific winter cruise, or you can embark on a round Britain cruise, in a cosy little ship, that offers simple comfort in return for a very modest fare. There is what might be described as the classic cruise, a two or three week jaunt, in a large, well found liner that normally plies on a regular scheduled service and had been diverted temporarily to undertake a cruise programme. On this type of classic cruise the emphasis is heavily on entertainment of all kinds: dancing, cabaret, cinema shows, horse racing, bingo, galas, deck sport competitions and all this is laid on for the delectation of the passenger. Ports of call are frequent, and the itinerary has been carefully thought out, to ensure variety. A full programme of shore expeditions will also be available.

Cruising is travel without tears as everything is taken care of by experienced hands. Incidentally, those who hate organised entertainment and only want to be left in peace are also probably best suited to a large liner as there is always somewhere on such a ship where one may settle, quietly, in a deck chair away from the maddening crowds. The smaller the ship the more difficult it is to get away. Next comes a cruise in a smaller ship, which has probably been specially designed for cruising. In the summer, she may ply in Northern Waters; in the spring and autumn she may, perhaps, turn her bows towards the warmer waters of the Mediterranean.

Then there are the specialist cruises, of which the archaeological cruise is a popular example. Archaeological cruises are normally accompanied by guest lecturers, who are expert in their fields of scholarship. In home waters, there are Islands and Gardens cruises. A ship is especially chartered, and the itineraries are enticing, wandering as they do through the western isles of Scotland, and around the sea lochs that run deep into the mainland. Another good opportunity in home waters is a cruise from London to Dublin and Liverpool, with possible calls at Cork and Belfast, returning to London via Southampton. The average duration of this cruise is ten days and fares are moderate. There are many cruise holidays afloat, along the canals and inland waterways of Britain, one can cruise in a cargo ship or book a round voyage on a regular passenger service. The range is vast. At the end of the journey you will have experienced the joys of being on a ship; the wonderful sense of ordered discipline, of a vast organisation ticking over remorseless, undeviating efficiency. You will have been part of the great and wonderful world of those who go down to the sea in ships, which is one of life's richest experiences.

Although the cruise industry has changed dramatically since those days, the basic tenants of cruising have remained the same since Elizabeth Nicholas wrote her article nearly fifty years ago. The ships have grown in size, the shipboard activities have expanded, and the choice of destination has increased, but the type of cruise and the experience of being on holiday at sea have remained the same. It is still possible to pick up your brochures from the local travel agent and search through to find your ideal vacation, deciding on the type of cabin and how many local tours to go on at the various ports that appeal to you. You may join the ship at a British port or decide to fly to the Mediterranean or Caribbean, or to extend the number of days spent in the sun by booking a hotel at the beginning or end of your cruise.

The early years of the new century have seen the introduction of the mega cruise ship, which is able to carry over 4,000 passengers on each cruise. The entertainment on board includes golf, rock climbing, race car driving, ice skating and trapeze. You can participate in pool games, compete in basketball and volleyball tournaments or take dance lessons. Indoors, you may prefer a history lecture, cards or bingo, napkin-folding or flower arranging, auctions, cooking demonstrations or wine tasting. Alternatively, you can ignore all of the organised activities and sunbathe at the pool with a cocktail.

The Passenger Shipping Association (PSA) statistics for 2009 showed that 1.53 million British people took a cruise holiday in 2008, which was 4 per cent higher than the previous year. They also found that cruising accounted for 10.6 per cent of the overseas package holidays market. In 1997, less than 3 per cent of packaged holidays booked were cruises. Also in 2008, 60 per cent of passengers took more than one cruise a year. Passengers were cruising for longer, from an average of ten nights in 2008 to eleven in 2009. Bookings for luxury cruises were up by 50 per cent, with 31,000 people paying more than £5,000 for each cruise, and another 200,000 spending between £2,500 and £5,000. The PSA also found that a record of 591,000 passengers took cruises from the United Kingdom in 2009, giving the reason that it was convenient to pack the car with luggage and drive to the port, where there are no airport security problems and no delays.

The PSA survey for 2010 showed that the Mediterranean continued to be the most popular destination, with 43 per cent of British holidaymakers choosing to cruise there, which was an 18 per cent increase on the previous year. It also found that 653,000 people chose to sail from a British port, and that fly-cruises had increased by 3 per cent to 968,000.

The market has continued to grow on both sides of the Atlantic, with new and larger ships being added to operator's fleets each year. It is claimed that entertainment is of a professional standard, equal to that found in theatres and entertainment centres ashore. Casinos are popular, with slot machines, poker or blackjack. Lounges feature live bands and cabaret singers with piano bars and karaoke. Broadway shows are produced, and singers, magicians, comedians and internationally known artists perform in the theatre each night. Large screens are provided, and show outdoor movies on the pool deck at night; parents can leave their children with trained youth counsellors, who lead them in organised games, contests, hunts, art and craft projects and supervised play.

However, the very short turnarounds can create major difficulties when a problem arises. Most cruise ships arrive in the port early in the morning at the end of the cruise, and the crew have a very short time to prepare the vessel for their next guests, who are usually boarding the same afternoon. A mechanical problem can delay the ship, and the time it takes to rectify can alter the schedule of ports visited during the cruise. Some delays mean that certain ports of call are cancelled, and passengers have to be refunded part or the whole of their cruise fare. Another major problem experienced is the outbreak of shipboard disease or viruses, which soon spread around the vessel. Most are minor and can be contained, but there have been examples where hundreds of passengers have been affected. Not only can this affect the current cruise, but it can also delay the sailing for the next group of passengers, as it may be necessary to clean and disinfect the vessel before she is able to sail again.

Dunera was built in 1937 for the British-India Steam Navigation Company. On 10 July 1940 Italian and German 'enemy aliens' were embarked on *Dunera* at Liverpool to be deported to Australia. The ship arrived at Sydney, and the appalling conditions experienced by the passengers became known. On arrival they set up their own community and when the Japanese attacked Pearl Harbor later in the war the prisoners were declassified as 'friendly aliens'. The community set up at Hay in New South Wales is marked by a plaque saying:–

> This plaque marks the 50th anniversary of the arrival from England of 1,984 refugees from Nazi oppression, mistakenly shipped out on HMT 'Dunera' and interned in Camps 7 & 8 on this site from 7. 9. 1940 to 20. 5. 1941. Many joined the AMF on their release from internment and made Australia their homeland and greatly contributed to its development. Donated by the Shire of Hay – September 1990.

Dunera was later involved in operations in Madagascar, Scilly and Southern France, and in 1945 she transported occupation personnel to Japan, after the Japanese surrender. She became a troopship in 1951, and in 1960 she was converted to an educational cruise ship. She operated in this role for the next seven years and was sold and broken up in Bilbao.

Nevasa was built by Barclay Curle as a troop transport, and was delivered to the British India Line on 12 July 1956. When the troop service ended in 1962 she was laid up in the River Fal.

British India Educational cruises, 1970. The educational cruises were advertised as offering free jet air transfer when shown in the programme and no baggage restrictions, no port taxes or passenger dues to pay, free shore excursions, all the year round operation, wide choice of itineraries, cruises from many major UK ports, illustrated travel talks by experts, fascinating inshore cruising, and a relaxed, friendly and informal atmosphere. The educational cruises varied in duration from ten to twenty-eight days and included calls at most of the major ports of Europe, Scandinavia, North Africa and Asia Minor, as well as a number of unusual places off the main tourist routes. There were also occasional cruises farther afield to West Africa and the West Indies. Pupils were supervised by staff from their own schools and all came under the control of the ship's permanent educational staff. Consequently, many thousands of British school children benefited from this unique form of educational travel, and the success and development of the scheme was partly due to the support received from the many Local Education Authorities who were impressed by this method of seeing geography and history and practising modern languages. It was also possible to arrange special cruises for specific groups and people with a particular interest. *Nevasa* and *Uganda* had separate accommodation for independent adult passengers. This included a range of public rooms; the majority of the cabins had private showers and toilets, and many were air-conditioned. The public rooms included the dining room, drawing room, smoke room and writing room. There were separate decks reserved for the cabin passengers and they also had their own private heated swimming pool. Cabin passengers could also attend the various lectures, join free shore excursions and take part in many of the activities aboard.

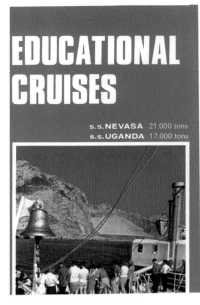

EDUCATIONAL CRUISES

s.s. **NEVASA** 21,000 tons
s.s. **UGANDA** 17,000 tons

The Ships

	Nevasa	Uganda
Tonnage	21,000	17,000
Length	609 ft.	540 ft.
Dormitory Berths	1,090	920
Cabin Berths (for adult passengers including party leaders).	307	304

Both ships are of British registry and have anti-roll stabilising equipment.

Both Ships

The educational facilities provided in *Nevasa* and *Uganda*, some of which are listed below, have been developed and improved through eight years of experience in the field of educational travel. They will not be found in any other ships afloat today. Each ship's company, of nearly 400 Officers and Ratings, includes the permanent education staff who give the introductory lectures in the assembly hall and advise Party Leaders on the best means of using the opportunities offered by the ship's facilities and the cruise itself.

Classrooms – 17 in "Nevasa"; 14 in "Uganda"
Refectory with Cafeteria Service
Assembly Hall seating over 400 students with full stage facilities and cinema projection
Ample Deck Space for physical education and games
Dispensary and Hospital Wards
Comfortable Dormitories (with adjacent washing and lavatory facilities) – supervised by Matrons and Masters-at-Arms

Map and Information Room	*Student Common Rooms*
Heated Swimming Pool	*Photographic Room*
Tuck Shop	*Hair-Drying Room*
Laundrettes	*Library*

Nevasa was converted in 1965 by Barclay Curle to an educational cruise ship, at a cost of nearly £1 million. She had accommodation for 1,100 pupils and separate accommodation for 307 cabin passengers, including the teaching staff accompanying the pupils. *Uganda* was converted in 1967 at a cost of nearly £3 million and she could accommodate 920 pupils, and also had accommodation for 304 cabin-class passengers. She was broken up in 1975.

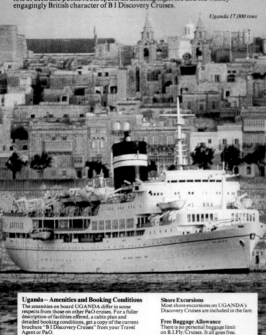

B.I. Discovery Cruises

Greek Islands, Turkey, the Holy Land and Egypt November '77-May '78

When you take a Discovery Cruise aboard 'UGANDA' you are one of only 300 passengers. The atmosphere is friendly, cheerful and relaxing, embracing the pleasures of cruising but putting a particular importance on the places to be seen. For these cruises are planned for their historic and geographic interest. Also aboard are students, who travel quite separately from you. And if you wish you can attend their illustrated lectures given by experts.

You enjoy excellent service, a good table and wine list, a comfortable cabin, lots of deck and public room space, an amusing night life and the wholly engagingly British character of B I Discovery Cruises.

Uganda 17,000 tons

Uganda—Amenities and Booking Conditions
The amenities on board UGANDA differ in some respects from those on other P&O cruises. For a fuller description of facilities offered, a cabin plan and detailed booking conditions, get a copy of the current brochure "B I Discovery Cruises" from your Travel Agent or P&O.

Shore Excursions
Most shore excursions on UGANDA's Discovery Cruises are included in the fare.

Free Baggage Allowance
There is no personal baggage limit on B.I.Fly/Cruises. It all goes free.

B+I Discovery Cruises, 1977.

B·I

TO EAST AFRICA

S.S. "UGANDA"
LONDON
FOR
GIBRALTAR, ADEN, MOMBASA, ZANZIBAR, DAR ES SALAAM, BEIRA & DURBAN

(Refrigerated space available)

LOADING AT	PORTS OF CALL	DUE	RECEIVING DATES
21 Shed,	*GIBRALTAR - - -	18 Nov.	5/12 Nov.
Royal	ADEN - - - -	27 Nov.	
Albert	MOMBASA - - -	2 Dec.	
Dock,	ZANZIBAR - - -	7 Dec.	
London.	DAR ES SALAAM -	8 Dec.	5/9 Nov.
	BEIRA - - - -	12 Dec.	
	DURBAN - - -	16 Dec.	

*On P & O Berth.

With liberty to call at other ports on or off the route.
Subject to alteration or cancellation without notice.

All cargo should be booked with Gellatly Hankey & Co. Ltd., One Aldgate, E.C.3 (Telephone ROYal 7364).

General enquiries regarding sailings may also be made with the British India Steam Navigation Co. Ltd., One Aldgate, E.C.3 (Telephone ROYal 4535).

For conditions, etc., see overleaf.

Uganda sailing list. Details of *Uganda*'s 'liner' service to South Africa prior to her being converted to an educational cruise ship.

Canberra, 1977.

P&O's *Strathmore*.

QE2 New World cruises

Cruise to New York, cruise home free!

Here's a new concept, a new way to experience cruising at it's most glamorous and sophisticated; 10 or 11-day round-trip voyages to New York and back on the greatest ship in the world, Queen Elizabeth 2.

And there's a tremendous bonus which makes it doubly attractive. **You pay only for the one-way Atlantic crossing; the other way is on us, absolutely free!** The same cabin, the same restaurant, all the superb QE2 facilities and entertainment are yours for the return trip as our guest. It's an opportunity too exceptional to miss.

More than that, you've a full day in New York to spend as you will. A whole day sightseeing and shopping tour that includes all the major attractions is included, but you can plan your own programme if you prefer.

Choose from any of eight dates, from spring to autumn, in 1979.

	Southampton Sail 11.30am	Cherbourg 6.30-8pm	New York 8am-7pm	Cherbourg 5pm-7pm	Southampton Arrive 8am	
1	May 14	May 14	May 19	May 24	May 25	12 days from £505
2	May 26	May 26	May 31	–	Jun 5*	11 days from £505
3	Jun 6†	Jun 6†	Jun 11	Jun 16	Jun 17	12 days from £535
4	Jul 18	Jul 18	Jul 23	Jul 28	Jul 29	12 days from £535
5	Aug 19	Aug 19	Aug 24	–	Aug 29*	11 days from £535
6	Sep 8	Sep 8	Sep 13	Sep 18	Sep 19	12 days from £505
7	Sep 20	Sep 20	Sep 25	Sep 30	Oct 1	12 days from £505
8	Oct 2	Oct 2	Oct 7	–	Oct 12*	11 days from £505

*Arrive 4.30pm   †See page 6 for departure times on this date

QE2 New World cruises, 1979.

Oriana.

We discover Cruising

P&O

P&O Cruising advertisement.

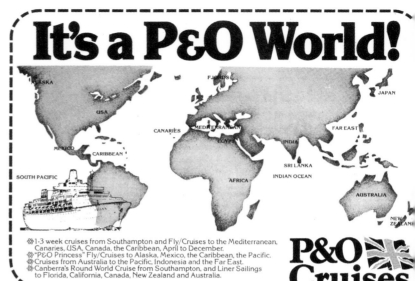

It's a P&O World!

❋ 1-3 week cruises from Southampton and Fly/Cruises to the Mediterranean, Canaries, USA, Canada, the Caribbean, April to December.
❋ "P&O Princess" Fly/Cruises to Alaska, Mexico, the Caribbean, the Pacific.
❋ Cruises from Australia to the Pacific, Indonesia and the Far East.
❋ Canberra's Round World Cruise from Southampton, and Liner Sailings to Florida, California, Canada, New Zealand and Australia.

P&O Cruises

P&O Cruises advertisement, 1979.

Saxonia became *Leonid Sobinov*.

Leonid Sobinov

21,400 tons

She is, despite her name, a ship of British origin, built in the John Brown Shipyard on the Clyde. In 1973, she was purchased by the Black Sea Shipping Co. and renamed the 'Leonid Sobinov' after the famous Russian opera singer. One class, stabilised, with all kinds of amenities – swimming pool, 5 bars, cinema, restaurant, ballroom, 'disco', library, plus English & Russian shops, and with air conditioning in public rooms. For the past 3 years she has been cruising with CTC as well as voyaging to Australia and New Zealand.

Cabins. A wide and varied selection to choose from – all air-cooled, roomy, comfortable and pleasantly decorated. Most have their own facilities with bath or shower and WC.

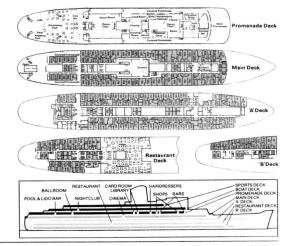

Plan of *Leonid Sobinov*.

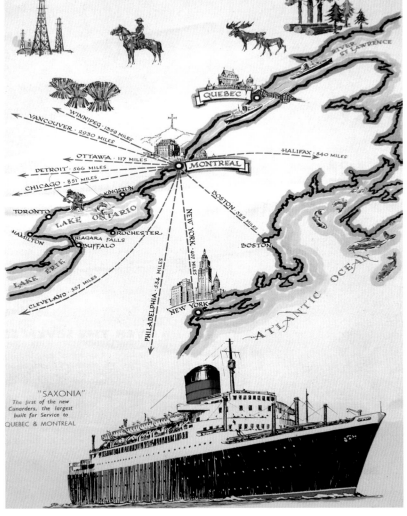

Saxonia.

Island Princess.

Christening of *Star Princess* on 23 March 1989 by the film star Audrey Hepburn, at a dockside ceremony at Port Everglades in Fort Lauderdale. The Band of Her Majesty's Royal Marines, specially flown over for the event, played a selection of music, and the theme music from the *Love Boat* television series. This was followed by a benediction by the Reverend Bishop James Duncan, and 15,000 balloons were released above the ship.

Princess Cruises' crew said farewell to the *Sun Princess* when she was officially handed over to her new owners, Premier Cruise Line, at the end of February 1989. The flag changing ceremony took place when Captain Chris Sample lowered the British flag, and in turn the ship's new master, Captain Dimitrios Chilas, raised the Bahamian flag in its place. Since her maiden voyage with Princess, she had carried over 460,000 passengers and sailed over almost a million and a half nautical miles, using 305,000 tons of fuel oil.

North Sea Ferries' *Norsea*.

Coast Lines' *Scottish Coast* becomes *Galaxias* at Birkenhead in 1969. *Scottish Coast* was built for Coast Lines' Irish Sea services and was sold in 1969 and renamed *Galaxias*. She was used as a floating hotel at Vancouver in 1986 and became *Princesa Amorosa* in 1989. She was broken up in 2002.

Orpheus, in 1990, was originally the British & Irish vessel *Munster*; when she was replaced by a drive-on/drive-off car-ferry she was sold and converted into a cruise ship. She was renamed *Theseus*, *Orpheus*, *Orpheu*, and was broken up in 2001. *Orpheus* was described as an attractive, welcoming ship, large enough to provide spacious living on board, yet small enough to enter harbours often denied to larger vessels. She was comfortably furnished and efficiently run with air-conditioned cabins, all of which had private facilities. Amenities aboard included a library, swimming pool, hairdresser, shop and laundry, and a doctor was available on each cruise.

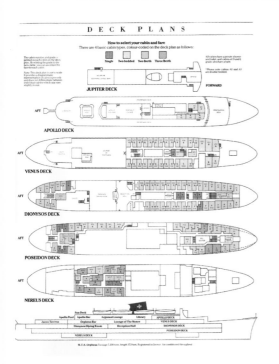

Plan of *Odysseus*. *Odysseus* was launched as *Leinster* for the B+I line's service from Liverpool to Dublin. She was transferred to the Belfast route in 1946 and renamed *Ulster Prince*. In 1966 she was replaced by a new car-ferry of the same name and she became *Ulster Prince 1*. She was sold to the Epirotiki Steam Ship Company in 1968, becoming *Adria* and *Odysseus* in 1969. She returned to Britain to be laid up, arriving at Glasgow on 22 July 1977, and was sold to Shipbreaking Industries at Faslane, where she arrived on 2 October 1979.

Cruise-Awhile, Stay-Awhile

8 days from £57.6s.
15 days from £76.6s.

Departing Saturdays 8, 15, 22, 29 May; 5, 12, 19, 26 June; 3, 10, 17, 24, 31 July; 7, 14, 21, 28 August; 4, 11, 18, 25 September; 2, 9, 16, 23 October 1971 on M.T.S. Odysseus.
Holiday Number KK 12.

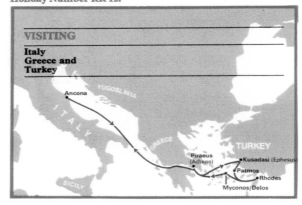

VISITING
**Italy
Greece and
Turkey**

Cruise Schedule.

Ulster Prince I.

Caledonian MacBrayne's *Hebridean Isles.*

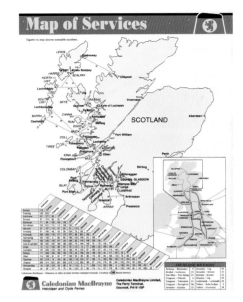

Caledonian MacBrayne Map of
Services, 1993.

Caledonian MacBrayne's *Lord of the Isles.*

Introducing Princess Voyages' *Crown Princess* in 1990. She became *A'Rosa Blu* in 2002, *AIDAblu* in 2004, *Ocean Village* in 2007 and *Pacific Jewel* in 2009.

Introducing Princess Cruises' *Grand Princess*, 1998.

Queen Elizabeth 2, 1986. The cruise programme brochure detailed the facilities offered on *Queen Elizabeth 2*, which included the Club Lido, the Golden Door Health Spa and the Computer Learning Centre: 'Here you can learn about software and hardware, VDU's and keyboards and find it fun. You can also take on our chess wizard (it's a computer) or play the latest computer games.'

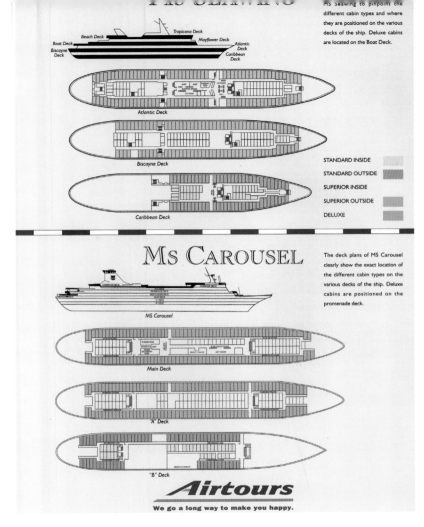

MS Seawing to pinpoint the different cabin types and where they are positioned on the various decks of the ship. Deluxe cabins are located on the Boat Deck.

Boat Deck
Biscayne Deck
Beach Deck
Tropicana Deck
Mayflower Deck
Atlantic Deck
Caribbean Deck

Atlantic Deck

Biscayne Deck

STANDARD INSIDE
STANDARD OUTSIDE
SUPERIOR INSIDE
SUPERIOR OUTSIDE
DELUXE

Caribbean Deck

MS CAROUSEL

The deck plans of MS Carousel clearly show the exact location of the different cabin types on the various decks of the ship. Deluxe cabins are positioned on the promenade deck.

MS Carousel

Main Deck

"A" Deck

"B" Deck

Airtours

We go a long way to make you happy.

Airtours' *Seawing* and *Carousel*.

Crown Jewel was built for Crown Cruise Line in 1992 and was chartered to Cunard Line the following year as *Cunard Crown Jewel*. She was sold to Star cruises and renamed *SuperStar Gemini* in 1995, to operate cruises from Singapore. It was reported that she had been sold to Jewel Owner Limited in 2008, who announced that she would be renamed *Vision Star*, and chartered to Vision Cruises. However, Vision Cruises ceased operations in 2009 and she was renamed *Gemini*, operated by the Quail Travel Group under the name *Happy Cruises*. She sailed on Caribbean cruises for them in 2010 but they ceased operations in September 2011 and *Gemini* was berthed in Tilbury Docks, at London.

Queen Elizabeth 2 in the River Mersey.

It is now possible to look at alternative cruises online, and make the bookings from the comfort of your own home. Some sites even allow you to take a tour of the vessel so that you are fully conversant with the position of your cabin, the dining facilities and the variety of entertainment offered before you even board the ship. Once you have paid your deposit, confirmation is sent to you and you can go ahead and make your plans for the cruising holiday. However, the days of the British cruise ship are limited, as there are now few vessels flying the Red Ensign.

The Cunard Line announced in 2011 that its passenger vessels would be registered in Bermuda, enabling it to take advantage of the lucrative market for weddings at sea, as these ceremonies are not recognised by British law. Consequently, Hamilton, Bermuda, replaced Southampton on the stern of *Queen Mary 2*, *Queen Victoria* and *Queen Elizabeth*.

Cunard claimed,

Most of our competitors have been developing increasingly popular and lucrative weddings at sea programmes and these are very big business in the cruise industry. We receive a lot of enquiries about the possibility of being married on one of our ships, particularly about weddings in the mid-Atlantic on board *Queen Mary 2*, which no other company can offer.

The change of registry also allowed Cunard to avoid the United Kingdom's employment laws, as the introduction of the 2010 Equality Act meant that ships registered in Britain were required to pay all staff from European Union countries wages equal to those of British people.

There has been an increase in the popularity of cruise and resort packages, which enable passengers to combine a cruise with a holiday at a beach resort or hotel. The major package holiday companies in the United Kingdom offer this alternative to the traditional cruise by giving customers the opportunity to tailor a package to their individual needs, using the ship as their floating hotel in a different port every day, and offering a stay at the resort at the beginning or end of the cruise.

CruiseBritain figures released early in 2013 showed that 962,000 passengers began their cruise at a United Kingdom port in 2012, which was a 10 per cent increase on 2011; 84 per cent of passengers were British. Forty-seven different cruise lines included British ports in their 2012 schedules. CruiseBritain commented that 'since 2004, we have seen the number of visiting passengers more than double and the number of visiting cruise ships calling has gone from 76 to 105, a rise of 38 per cent'.

Sunbird entered service as *Song of America* in 1982, becoming *SunBird* in 1999 and *Thomson Destiny* in 2005. She was sold to Louis Cruise Lines in 2012, becoming *Louis Olympia*.

Shetland Weekend Mini-Cruises, 2000.

SHETLAND WEEKEND Mini-Cruises

Sample Ship-board life as you wine, dine, and dance your way to Shetland on board, your floating hotel

2 DAYS, 3 NIGHTS

On board your mini-cruise ship "St Clair", our friendly staff will do everything possible to ensure that you will have a memorable weekend. There's a first class restaurant where you'll enjoy our excellent cuisine – eight delicious meals commencing with dinner on sailing night, through to breakfast before disembarking – a bar and lounges where you can relax, or dance to the music provided, as well as comfortable cabins. There's a shop too and feature films shown each evening.

Departing Aberdeen Fridays at 1800 hrs arriving in Lerwick Saturdays at 0800 hrs. Return sailing from Lerwick on Sundays at 1800 hrs to arrive back in Aberdeen Mondays at 0800 hrs.

COACH TOURS – On Shetland we offer excellent "value for money" coach tours as an optional extra. They are bookable on board ship at the Purser's Office and normally the following tours are available:

SATURDAY – Morning and afternoon tours to Sumburgh and Jarlshof or Scalloway, Burra Isle and historical sites.

SUNDAY – All day tours to Hillswick or North Isles with lunch en route included.

WEEKEND MINI-CRUISE FARES			
FRIDAY DEPARTURES FROM ABERDEEN			
APRIL 14, 21, 28	MAY 5, 12, 26	JUNE 2, 16, 23	SEPTEMBER 1, 8, 15,
14 APRIL - 26 MAY		2 - 23 JUNE 1 - 15 SEPTEMBER	
ADULT*	£140	£170	
CHILD*	£85	£120	

ADULT* – Sharing 2 berth cabin with shower & toilet
Cabin with washbasin only – available at a reduction of £20 per adult, £10 per child
CHILD* – 4 and under 14 years (Infants under 4 years not occupying a berth - FREE)

P&O Scottish Ferries Cruises, 1998.

Eugenio Costa was completed in 1966 for Costa Line and is seen here as *Eugenio C.* She became *Edinburgh Castle* in 1998, when she was operating for Direct Cruises on cruises from United Kingdom ports. She then became *Big Red Boat II*, and was broken up in 2005 at Alang.

Edinburgh Castle at Liverpool.

Cunard Countess, 1990. Cunard claimed that of all the ships cruising in the Caribbean, she was the only vessel that brought the full complement of eleven different Caribbean islands in just two weeks, and even the one-week cruise offered a choice of six or seven islands to be explored in only seven days. She became *Awani Dream 2* in 1996, *Olympic Countess* in 1998, *Olympia Countess* in 2002, *Ocean Countess* in 2004, *Marleen* in 2005, *Lili Marleen* in 2006, *Ocean Countess* in 2006, *Ruby* in 2007 and *Ocean Countess* in 2007. On 30 November 2013 she suffered a serious fire in Chalkis in Greece, and it was found that she was uneconomic to repair, so she was broken up in 2014.

Royal Viking Sun was built for the Royal Viking Line and became part of the Cunard fleet when the Line were taken over in 1994. *Royal Viking Sun* was transferred to Seabourn, renamed *Seabourn Sun* in 1999, and *Prinsendam* in 2002, operating for the Holland America Line.

The *Sylvania* as *Fairwind* in 1987. She became *Fairwind* in 1968, *Sitmar Fairwind* and *Dawn Princess* in 1988, *Albatros* in 1993 and *Genoa* in 2004, when she was broken up at Alang.

Vistafjord, 1998. *Vistafjord* was renamed *Caronia* at Liverpool Pier Head on 10 December 1999, becoming *Saga Ruby* in 2005 and *Oasia* in 2014.

Fairwind, 1987.

Above: The Cunard liner *Sylvania* as *Albatros*. She is shown here in the River Mersey on a 'Round Britain Cruise'.

Above: Fairwind in the Panama Canal.

Right: Aurora in the Panama Canal, 2006.

P&O's *Aurora* and *Oriana* world cruises, 2001.

THINKING ABOUT A NEW ITINERARY? Thinking about how to make your cruise extra special for your passengers? Start thinking about Greenock Ocean Terminal, conveniently located for itinerary planning and the perfect gateway to Scotland.

With a quayside length of 367m and a draft of 12.6m, the port boasts excellent facilities, a magnificent scenic approach and an enviable level of service.

- it just goes to prove we've thought of everything.

From the fascinating history and heritage of the local area, to the vibrancy and cosmopolitan ambience of Glasgow, Greenock Ocean Terminal offers a tremendous wealth of excursion options to suit all tastes. Whether your passengers are looking for culture, scenery, historic sites, excitement or relaxation - it's all here.

A trip to the world-renowned Burrell Collection, home to Rodin's "The Thinker" is well worth thinking about!

Main picture: Rodin's "The Thinker" at The Burrell Collection
Inset (left to right): House for an Art Lover, Glasgow; Pipers at Greenock Ocean Terminal, The Cloch Lighthouse, Inverclyde; Princes Square, Glasgow

For more information please contact:

ELAINE DICKIE
Sales Manager - Leisure Tourism,
Greater Glasgow & Clyde Valley Tourist Board,
11 George Square, Glasgow G2 1DY
Tel: +44 (0) 141 204 4480 Fax: +44 (0) 141 204 4772
Web: www.seeglasgow.com

PETER SOMMERVILLE
Operations Manager,
Greenock Ocean Terminal,
Partick Street, Greenock PA16 8UU
Tel: +44 (0) 1475 726 171 Fax: +44 (0) 1475 888 130

Cruise Greenock advertisement, 2001.

Aurora leaves Sydney on her maiden world cruise in 2001.

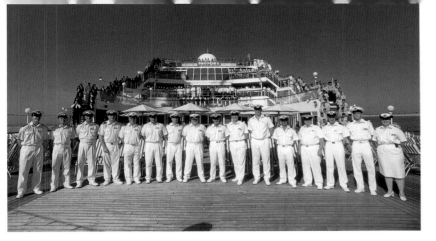

Saga Ruby, 2002.

Saga Ruby World Cruise, 2001.

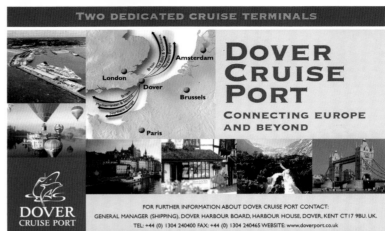

Dover Cruise Port advertisement, 2001.

Pacific Princess was built as *R Three* for Renaissance Cruises in 1999. She was purchased by P&O Princess Cruises in 2002 and renamed *Pacific Princess*.

Top left: Spirit of Adventure was built as *Berlin* for Peter Deilmann in 1981. She was chartered by the Blue Funnel Line in 1982 to replace the *Centaur*, which operated from Singapore to Australia, and was renamed *Princess Mahsuri*, becoming *Berlin* again in 1984, when the charter was completed. In 2005 she operated on another charter as *Orange Melody* and became part of the Saga fleet at the end of 2005, being renamed *Spirit of Adventure*.

Left: Pacific Sky was built in 1984 for Sitmar Cruises and was named *Fairsky*. When Sitmar was purchased in 1988 by P&O she became *Sky Princess* and was allocated to the Princess Cruises fleet. P&O transferred her to P&O Cruises Australia in 2000 and she was renamed *Pacific Sky*, replacing *Fair Princess*. She was transferred to Pullmantur Cruises in 2006 as *Sky Wonder* for cruises in the Mediterranean. She was laid up at Piraeus in 2009 and sold and renamed *Atlantic Star* later that year. She was sold to the Kyma Ship Management Company in 2010 and was laid up at Marseille until 2013, when she was broken up at Aliaga, as *Antic*.

P&O Premium Pacific, 2003.

Pacific Princess, 2004.

Andrew Weir 'Cruise in style on board a freighter', 2004.

Victoria was originally the Swedish American Line passenger liner *Kungsholm*, and was built by John Brown & Company on the Clyde in 1966. She became *Sea Princess* in 1979, *Victoria* in 1995, *Mona Lisa* in 2002, *Oceanic II* in 2007, *Mona Lisa* again in 2008 and *Veronica* in 2010. As *Veronica* she is operating as a luxury floating hotel in the Sultanate of Oman, owned by DSME (Daewoo Shipbuilding & Marine Engineering).

Adonia was named by Miss Zara Phillips, and *Oceana* by Her Royal Highness, The Princess Royal in a joint ceremony on 21 May 2003.

Arcadia was originally laid down as a Holland America vessel, and later she was intended to be *Queen Victoria*, but was launched as owned by P&O. She is based in Southampton, cruising to the Mediterranean, northern Europe and around the British Isles. She is also scheduled to take a world cruise each year alongside other vessels in the fleet. During a major refit in 2008 she was fitted with additional cabins at her stern.

Carousel was built in 1971 as Nordic Queen, the second ship for the Royal Caribbean Line. She was purchased by Sun Cruises in 1995 and renamed Carousel. She was sold to Louis Cruise Lines in 2004 and chartered back to Sun Cruises until May the following year. In 2005 she was renamed Aquamarine and chartered to Transocean Tours as Arielle in 2006, reverting to Aquamarine again in 2008. She was sold to Ocean Star Cruises in 2010 and she was renamed Ocean Star Pacific.

Hebridean Spirit.

Sundream 2000. She was built in 1970 and was originally Song of Norway, becoming Sundream in 1997, Dream Princess in 2004, Dream in 2006, Clipper Pearl in 2007, Clipper Pacific in 2008, Festival in 2009, Ocean Pearl in 2010 and Formosa Queen in 2013. She was broken up in China in 2014.

Port of Tyne cruise advertisement, 2009.

Lounge on *Hebridean Princess*.

Milford Haven Cruise Port, 2001.

Queen Mary 2 in the Mersey.

Passengers enjoy the Mersey sunshine on *Queen Mary 2*'s visit to Liverpool on 15 September 2011.

Merseyside Maritime Museum

Open late
20 October till 8pm

To celebrate Queen Mary II
visit to Liverpool

Live music with The Shakers
Special talks on galleries

Maritime Dining Rooms (see over)
4th Floor special two course dinner menu
Also open for lunch and afternoon teas
Bar open

Table bookings: 0151 478 4056
Information desk: 0151 478 4499

FREE ENTRY   NATIONAL MUSEUMS LIVERPOOL

Merseyside Maritime Museum details for celebrating *Queen Mary 2*'s visit to Liverpool on 20 October 2009.

Top left: Queen Mary 2.

Top right: Queen Mary 2 lounge.

Left: Queen Mary 2 main staircase.

Liverpool Pier Head from a liner in the 1960s, above, and *Queen Mary 2*, below, in 2011.

A different kind of
CRUISING

A cruise on cargo passenger liner RMS *St Helena* is a voyage in the truest sense —
a chance to re-discover the joys of time and ultimately to explore a naturalist's paradise

St Helena, 2009.

St Helena at Cape Town. *St Helena* was built in 1990 to provide lifeline passenger and cargo services to the British Dependency of St Helena, a tiny island within the tropic of Capricorn in the South Atlantic. Sailing on *St Helena* has been described as an unforgettable experience, with a lifestyle reminiscent of the great liners of the past: relaxing on the sun deck, traditional entertainment, excellent food and wine, impeccable service and an ever-changing ocean. From 2005 she has operated from Cape Town to the island, with only two voyages a year from the United Kingdom. The voyage from Britain is approximately 6,000 miles and calls at Tenerife and Ascension Island. She carries 1,500 tons of cargo and 128 passengers. She is fitted with modern passenger accommodation; there is a shop, a purser's bureau, which acts as a bank, a post office and international telephone exchange and a publisher of the ship's daily newspaper. There is a doctor on board with a small hospital, and a laundry, and all cabins have air conditioning, private facilities and an open view of the ocean.

P&O's *Pride of Le Havre* provided cruises on the Portsmouth–Le Havre service from 1994 to 2005 to 'explore the delights of Normandy or venture into the beautiful Pays d'Auge, land of Camembert and Calvados or the old world charm of Rouen and picturesque Honfleur'. In 2005 she was laid up on the River Fal, and in November that year she was sold to SNAV and renamed *SNAV Sardegna*, for the service from Civitavecchia to Palermo and Olbia.

Right: P&O Spain Mini-Cruise, 2009. P&O introduced the service from Portsmouth to Bilbao by *Pride of Bilbao* in April 1993. The service operated twice weekly, leaving Portsmouth on Wednesdays and Sundays and Bilbao on Mondays and Thursdays. The voyage took approximately twenty-eight hours and was described and advertised as a mini-cruise. *Pride of Bilbao* offered saunas, pools, solarium, conference rooms, restaurants and bars, and berths for 2,400 passengers in cabins and suites.

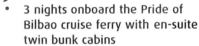

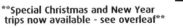
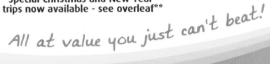

Above: Saga Rose *and* Saga Ruby.

Top left: Saga Rose.

Left: Saga Cruises' *Saga Pearl II* in 2010. In May 2012 she became *Quest for Adventure.*

Princess Cruises' *Crown Princess* was built in two sections. The aft section was constructed at the Fincantieri yard in Monfalcone while the forward section came from the Sestri yard at Genoa. She sailed from New York on her maiden voyage on 14 June 2006, and a month later a mistake by one of her officers caused a severe list, which resulted in many passengers and crew being injured. She sails on cruises from Fort Lauderdale and Galveston, then on southern, western and eastern Caribbean cruises in the winter. Cruises to the Mediterranean, Scandinavia, northern Europe and around the British Isles are offered in the summer.

Caribbean Princess at Liverpool on a 'Round Britain' cruise. She was built by Fincantieri and was originally intended to be a P&O vessel. However, she was introduced into the Princess Cruises fleet as *Caribbean Princess*, initially for service in the Caribbean.

Princess Cruises' *Royal Princess* and her sister *Regal Princess* entered service in 2013–14. The Horizon Court offers 900 indoor and 350 outdoor seats, and is transformed at night into the Horizon Bistro. The Piazza atrium on *Royal Princess* was expanded to serve as a social hub, offering quick meals, beverages, entertainment, shopping and guest services. The Vines wine bar serves a selection of regional snacks, and the adjacent Sabatini's is a Tuscan-inspired speciality restaurant. The Symphony Dining Room is aft of the Piazza with the Lotus Spa and saloon, offering a hydrotherapy pool and thermal suite. The forward section of Decks 6 and 7 encompasses the 1,000-seat Princess Theatre, and aft of this is the Casino and Night Club. In the adjacent Piazza is the new concept of the Italian-inspired Bellini Bar and Alfredo's Pizzeria. On Deck 7 there is the Crooners Bar, Ocean Terrace and Seafood Bar. Further aft is Princess Live, seating 276 passengers; the television studio is a first for a Princess ship. Passengers are able to watch live cookery demonstrations, game shows, late-night comedy and small-scale performances by the ship's musicians. There is also the Vista Lounge, Fountain Pool, Plunge Pool and an adults-only sanctuary with its own pool. The fitness centre incorporates a state-of-the-art gym with ocean views, and there is the Princess Sports Central, which is a multi-sport area comprising court games, lawn activities and a lounge for virtual gaming.

ENTERTAINMENT

1 Broadway Show Lounge: West End-style musicals and comedy from UK guest acts are staged in this two-storey show lounge.

2 Medusa Lounge: Live bands, game shows and spotlight cabaret take to the floor here.

3 The Water's Edge: This venue is home to karaoke, cabaret and, of course, the dance floor.

Argo Lounge: Live classical music sets a relaxing scene in this laid-back venue.

Casino: Roulette, blackjack and slot machines are just a taste of what's in store in the casino.

DINING - WAITER SERVICE

4 Orion Restaurant: Offering breakfast, lunch and six-course dinners, this stylish waiter service eatery has an open-seating policy so you can dine where and when you like.

The Grill: A posh take on surf'n'turf is the house speciality at The Grill, where steaks, seafood and fresh fish are cooked to order. A cover charge applies and onboard reservations are required.

Gala night: The weekly Captain's Cocktail Party and Gala Dinner is an event worth dressing up for.

DINING - FLEXIBLE OPTIONS

5 Lido Restaurant: Help-yourself buffets. Plus there are themed nights twice a week.

Sirens Restaurant: Booths, tables for two and space for the whole family - Sirens offers the ideal setting for buffet breakfasts and lunches.

Terrace Grill: Lunchtime BBQs, pizzas and salads served in the sunshine.

Thomson Dream.

Empress of Britain was launched by Her Majesty Queen Elizabeth on 22 June 1955, and operated cruises for numerous owners and under various names until she was broken up at Alang in 2008. She became *Queen Anna Maria* in 1965, *Carnivale* in 1975, *Fiesta Marina* in 1993, *Olympic* in 1995 and the *Topaz* in 1997.

Olympic.

Carnivale.

Topaz.

Topaz as the 'Peace Boat'.

Balmoral arriving at Liverpool on the '*Titanic* Anniversary Cruise'. *Balmoral* was built for the Royal Cruise Line by Meyer at Papenburg in Germany as the *Crown Odyssey*. She became *Norwegian Crown* in 1996 and was purchased by Fred Olsen Lines in 2006. Following an overhaul in Hamburg and the fitting of a 30-metre section, she emerged as the *Balmoral* the following year. In 2008 she was employed on Mediterranean fly-cruises and was later based at Dover for a series of cruises from the United Kingdom.

Below right: Glen Massan sails from Oban. Both vessels operate Majestic Line Heritage and Wildlife cruises from Oban with the company describing the cruises thus:

Sailing on the lovingly restored vessels is a congenial and relaxed affair.

The size of the vessels allows inshore access to charming and remote areas not available to bigger cruise vessels.

Each day the vessels drop anchor at new destinations allowing guests the freedom to go ashore and explore alone or in groups.

Glen Tarsan at Oban.

There are many interesting historical places to visit and flora and fauna to observe both on land and at sea.

A high standard of hospitality is provided by the crew in a most unobtrusive way.

The amazing and dramatic scenery of Argyll is breath-taking

Fabulous meals with a focus on Argyll speciality produce.

Queen Elizabeth sails from the Mersey.

Queen Victoria on trials.

The Trinity House vessel *Patricia*.

Patricia Voyages, 'A Unique Experience', 2009. The Trinity House flagship *Patricia* carries passengers when she completes her work maintaining navigation buoys, refuelling lighthouses and marking wrecks around the United Kingdom coast. The cruise means that passengers can view her normal duties. She is fitted with six double cabins, and has a passenger chef and stewards to look after her passengers' needs. *Patricia* covers the coasts of England, Wales and the Channel Islands, and it is possible to put passengers ashore, subject to operational conditions. Harwich is her home base port but she calls regularly at other ports and harbours. You may have to join the ship from different places, and she may not always be alongside in port; joining and departing can occasionally be carried out via transfer by workboat.

Waverley anchored off Cammell Laird's yard on the Mersey. She is the last seagoing passenger-carrying paddle steamer in the world. *Waverley* was built in 1946 and sailed on cruises on the River Clyde until 1973. Following her withdrawal from service she was sold to the Paddle Steamer Preservation Society for a nominal fee. She is now owned by Waverley Excursions Limited and operates passenger excursions from ports around the British and Irish coast; she regularly sails from Glasgow and other places on the River Clyde, the Thames, the south coast of England, the Bristol Channel and the Isle of Man.

Balmoral also operated cruises for the Waverley Excursions Limited. However, she did not sail during 2013 and is laid up.